Ian Andrews

# Equipped
# to Heal

O&U
Onwards & Upwards
Publishers

Onwards and Upwards Publishers

Onwards and Upwards Publications
Berkeley House
11 Nightingale Crescent
West Horsley Surrey
KT24 6PD
England

www.onwardsandupwards.org

This edition published 2011
First Published 2002 USA

Cover photo provided by Stephen Matthews, Abundant Life Ministries , Bradford UK

ISBN: 978-1-907509-17-9

Cover design: Leah-Maarit

Printed in the UK

This is the best book I have read about the power of God to heal supernaturally. Ian clearly teaches that it is God's will to heal, and explains many different methods used by Jesus when here on earth. Ian's passion is not to tell you of the thousands healed under his ministry, but to equip you to tap into God's power and release healing into the lives of other people.

Ian stimulates your faith and boldness, but he also brings such a simplicity to his subject that you find yourself wanting to find someone who needs healing and pray for them. He does not dodge the issues of those who are not healed or when there is a long delay, and leaves no-one feeling that the reason they are not healed is due to lack of faith. Everyone who seeks to be used by God, and to pray for the sick, needs to read this book.

Charles Sibthorpe
The 222 Trust
2011

Not only has Ian seen miracles of biblical proportions, but he has also trained countless others to do likewise. For decades Ian has taught insights from the Old and New Testaments which are only now becoming widespread in the body of Christ. His teaching is both scriptural and practical. My shelves contain many half-read Christian books but this is one you'll read to the end. It's still my favourite book on healing.

Catherine Clark
The Healing Rooms
Oasis Church, London
April 2011

# Table of Contents

# Foreword

I am delighted to have been invited to write the foreword to Equipped to Heal by Ian Andrews. I first met Ian and his lovely wife, Rosemary, at a conference in Chard Guildhall in Somerset, England in May 1978. I was impressed with Ian's clear biblical teaching on the ministry of healing and the blending of Christ's compassion and the Holy Spirit's power in the way he and Rosemary prayed for the sick. In the years since, I have had many opportunities to be in meetings in which the Andrews have ministered. These meetings have ranged from home group meetings with a handful of people, to great conferences with many thousands present. I have observed in Ian steadfastness to his calling, consistency of results in healing, and integrity in ministry throughout the years. In my opinion, Ian Andrews is one of the most credible and balanced healing evangelists in the Body of Christ today. I have had the privilege of hosting and arranging healing meetings for the Andrews and have appreciated the friendship and partnership in the gospel that has developed.

Equipped to Heal combines a biblical-theological study of divine healing with the practical aspects of functioning in the ministry of healing. The emphasis in Ian's teaching ministry is to equip the members of the Body of Christ to effectively minister healing. When Ian conducted meetings at a church I pastored in Virginia, he taught and laid hands on our leaders and altar workers. Then he sent them throughout the congregation to minister to the sick. The results were spectacular.

There are many excellent books available on healing. However, many of these are based on the author's experience, with Scripture added to illustrate the points made. I am thrilled with Ian's book, which is based on exegesis of the Scriptures with regards to healing. Personal experiences are used to illustrate the truths derived from the exegesis. I am especially impressed by Ian's explanation of the relationship between the healing ministry and the government of God. Here he explains that the vital question to ask when you pray for someone to be healed is not, "Do I have faith?" but "Do I have authority?" By asking this and other questions, Ian puts the ministry of healing into the context of the current "Apostolic" Reformation.

Some of the most outstanding healing miracles that I have personally witnessed have taken place in meetings conducted by Ian Andrews. Over the years, I have personally benefited from and grown in my own ability to minister to the sick from Ian's teaching more than from any other healing minister. I enthusiastically commend Equipped to Heal to pastors, lay leaders, Bible college and seminary students, and to all believers who take Christ's command to his disciples seriously, when he said: "Heal the sick!"

Ian A. H. Bond, M.A., D.Min.
Executive Director and Dean
Christian Life School of Theology
Columbus, Georgia
January 2003

# Preface

Many years ago, when I was travelling and ministering in Sweden I received a word of prophecy that, over the years, my wife and I have tried to fulfil in our ministry. In the message I was given, God was asking me to build a mountain of men and women who will move in the power of God. And most of our teaching and healing ministry has been geared towards that end.

We have placed much more emphases in our meetings, on teaching others, raising up ministry teams and other fully-fledged competent healing ministries than in conducting large stadium-type healing services. The teaching has been well received in over sixty-five nations, and has resulted in many hundreds of healing ministries becoming effective throughout the world.

We were recently invited to bring this message to the Ukraine, and having taught in the Bible school there for a few days, we learned that after our departure, the Bible school students immediately put our teaching into practice. This resulted in four hundred people being healed and brought into the church on the following Sunday where they all gave their hearts to the Lord.

We sense that we are about to take another leap forward in our ministry training  program as I have recently been invited onto the faculty of many Bible schools and training centres around the world. I have been asked to head the International Association of Healing Ministries, a global network of healing ministries and  students and a part of the Resurrection Apostolic International Network, based in Minneapolis, MN. I am also providing the bulk of the teaching for the Apostolic Healing Institute's resources; I have developed Bible school courses and church and city-based healing seminars that can be taught around the world.

It is my hope and prayer that this book will act as a resource to enable your ministry to be enlarged and even more fruitful in the days of harvest that lie ahead.

Dr. Ian Andrews D.Min
www.ieequippers.org

January 2002 - 2011

# Introduction

There has not been a time in history when people's needs have been greater than they are today. We may think we have grown more sophisticated with our medical knowledge, scientific achievements, and material affluence, but all these have resulted in independence and self-sufficiency apart from God, which have led to broken relationships, wounded hearts, mental breakdowns, and all manner of illnesses. The devil is on the offensive in many people's lives, especially in the areas of sickness and disease, causing misery, pain, and suffering for many people. For this reason, we as God's people need to be thoroughly equipped and informed so that we can work effectively with God in carrying out His will to heal the sick and set the captives free in the name of Jesus.

Up until the '60s and early '70s, there were a few of God's people who were praying for the sick and seeing results. This seemed to happen more in America than in England. Perhaps it is because by nature we English are shy and reticent, so we were willing to stand back and let our American brothers and sisters step out of the boat into healing ministries. And so often in the past, they have given us an example of what God could and would do if we believed in Him.

I believe we are in a new day when God's Spirit is moving through all the earth in signs and wonders. He is raising up an army of men, women, and children through whom He can move to display His love and power to a broken and needy society; people who are just waiting to be shown what God's love is all about, not only with words but by a demonstration of His mercy in healing power.

God is not looking for success, for brilliance, or for head knowledge, but He is looking for volunteers, those of us who will say yes to Him. Use me Lord. We may feel weak and inadequate, but if we look at the way the Apostle Paul describes himself in the Book of Acts, we shall see that it was like that for him many times. Through experience though, he learned that when he let the Holy Spirit move through him, demonstrating the word of God, the results were mighty. There we see an amazing combination of the human and the divine: God putting His treasure, the Holy Spirit, into human beings. And that's the way He likes it, God and man working together. God uses our hands, our mouths, our bodies, and our minds. He allows us the thrill and joy of this experience, and yet we know that it is His power flowing through us as He does the healing. We all know that we couldn't heal a fly with a headache! Jesus said, "Apart from Me, you can do nothing," and in another instance He said, "The words I say to you are not just my own. Rather, it is the Father, living in Me, who is doing His work." We want to give credit where credit is due. All the credit for any healing goes to Jesus and all the glory to God the Father.

Jesus did, however, give us a great commission to "go into all the world and preach the gospel to every person"; "to heal the sick, set the demon possessed free, to heal those who are broken in spirit and hurting, and tell them the good news that the Kingdom of God has come" (Mark 16: 15-18). He has not only told us what to do, but has given us the power in the Holy Spirit and the authority in His name to carry it out. As we proclaim and teach this message of liberty, that the price to redeem man from suffering has already been paid in full by Jesus Himself, God says that He will confirm His word with signs and wonders and miracles.

How is this all going to come about? The needs are so great, the sicknesses so many and the workers so few.

We can change the course of this world by being changed ourselves and then being people-changers. You may not be able to change the whole world, but you can change somebody's world! We can do it together. Some of us will find ourselves called to a ministry instead of secular employment; some will be speaking to large crowds; some will function alongside others in the church, or take the church out onto the streets where the sick people are; some of us may be used with our neighbour or the person in our office at work. Everybody needs somebody, and that "somebody" is you and me. Jesus said to His disciples, "I chose you to go and bear fruit – fruit that will last." I remember a translation of this into pidgin English: Big Boss wants me and He thinks me good enough to do His work.

Don't wait, just volunteer. It's always nerve-racking to step out in faith for God. Look at Peter. He stepped out of the boat but then he panicked with fear when he looked down at the sea and began sinking. But Jesus immediately saved him and walked back with him to the boat. Peter had a lot to learn but he was willing, and instead of being a reed be became a rock in the church, and God did mighty things through him.

Our motive to see the sick healed is love. God so loved that He gave Jesus to die for sickness. We sometimes wonder if we've got it wrong when God heals those who (in our secret opinion) least qualify for healing! But God is a God of grace and love and has pity on those He has created, showing mercy to those who least deserve it.

We hope that you will be part of this vast army God is building to invade the territory of sickness, disease, and sin in Jesus' name. As you study and put into practice what you learn, then your faith will grow and things will begin to happen. God moves when we move. So let us go on, not having attained, but still learning – still pressing on to take hold of that prize which Christ Jesus won for us.

A few years ago, during a time of fellowship with friends, God spoke as we were praying about His will for the future in the ministry of healing. Someone saw a picture of a mountain, but instead of its usual rocky face, there were men and women packed tightly together, filling every space. The interpretation of the vision was that God wanted us to build a mountain of men and women who would be equipped to minister healing as a normal part of the message of God's grace whenever the opportunities occurred. Since then Ian and I have been holding training seminars where teaching and practice are the main emphases. The response from those attending has been very positive and folk have gone away with new vision, new confidence, and a definite biblical and spiritual authority for healing. They have left determined to put into practice what they have learned, in their homes, in the church and in evangelism. In fact, some have seen wonderful healings take place through them (much to their surprise!) and have begun to get a reputation for praying for the sick.

One important factor in this new move of God's Spirit is that He obviously intends both men and women to be involved in the healing ministry. Wherever a man is called to this work, it is of great benefit if his wife recognizes the invaluable contribution her own gifts and perspective give to the ministry. And, of course, if much travelling and living by faith is involved, then it helps if there is a mutual commitment to this calling. Another great advantage of establishing teamwork in the healing ministry is that we have seen, with much sadness, the pitfalls of one-man ministries. The pressures this situation puts on the individual are enormous, the dangers and temptations often unbearable: put on a pedestal by those who mistake the source of the ability and power demonstrated, they find themselves striving to live up to a reputation which at first may have seemed gratifying, or overwhelmed by the constant pressure to "perform" and deal with every problem of sickness they encounter. Often alone, isolated from family and fellowship while travelling, these men are subject to undue emotional and even moral problems through loneliness and opportunity, and frequently their own family life suffers. We who view these men as super-spiritual beings endowed with a special power have only ourselves to blame when we experience shock and disillusionment at their downfall. So wherever possible, we seek to encourage people to enter into this ministry in couples and teams, making sure our aim is to point people to God as the source of their health and teaching them to remain in and minister this life to others.

We have received a great encouragement in this vision recently. For a long time now, it has been in our hearts to bring this gift of God's healing to a far wider audience through the media. Previously, the door into television seemed to be firmly shut, although we felt somehow sure that this would eventually change, so we were very excited when Ian received a letter from BBC Scotland asking him to take part in one of a series of programs, called High Spirits, that they were doing on aspects of supernatural or miraculous movements within the church. The timing was ideal and fitted into our schedule perfectly. Our prompt reply was yes, provided the subject was to be treated in a sympathetic manner and allowed the viewing audience to make up its own mind as to the genuineness of God's power. Three other church leaders were invited for their opinions in order to give the necessary balance and credibility on the program.

The original uncut film took about six hours in front of a studio audience. It was pretty nerve-racking with technicians, cameramen and bright lights creating a very artificial setting. Would it work in such a clinical atmosphere? Suppose no one was healed! In spite of all our fears, God proved that this had indeed been His idea and He was about to show what He could do.

The first few words of knowledge were surprisingly alarming: they referred to someone who had been abused, perhaps, and had been afraid to tell anyone about it (What a way to start!). Amazingly, the girl responded and was wonderfully released. Faith began to rise as many others came forward to receive their healing following more words of knowledge, and it had a great effect on the television crew filming the scene. One cameraman remarked that this was the best religious program he had ever done. I suppose it was a little unusual!

Not surprisingly, we have had many inquiries following the program, some from people wondering if there would be any more healing "shows," a number from sick and depressed people asking for help, and our fair share of weird-and-wonderful letters. Many letters also came from Christians whose faith had been really encouraged and who felt the program had helped them in talking to others about healing. Plainly, there is an openness and thirst for the subject which was not present some years ago.

We are positive that there will be more opportunities in the future to bring the message of God's healing into people's homes through television so that people can turn to God rather than to other sources of help. Already we know of other Christians who have been approached to make programs on various aspects of God's healing, so things are on the move to demonstrate the infinite ability of God over the works of Satan. As we hold our city meetings, the ignorance and misconceptions concerning God's miraculous power are being broken down. God wants to use us all to bring in the light of His healing and His kingdom. Some of us will have a more specialized ministry and use certain gifts more than others, but the key word is involvement – be prepared to be used in any way in God's healing work – and to be involved you need understanding.

The understanding, or knowledge, that we need is revelation knowledge from God's Spirit to our spirits. He has promised to lead us into all truth (John 14:26) and to teach us all things concerning Himself. This kind of knowledge imparts life: it switches on the light inside and causes us to change in our thinking and actions – if we allow it. There is nothing so exciting as when Jesus shares Himself with us through His Word, just as He did with the disciples as they walked together on the Emmaus road. Didn't they say that their hearts burned within them as they talked along the way and Jesus shared about Himself from the Scriptures? They were kept from recognizing Him, but now God has given us His Holy Spirit so that we can know Him and the power of His resurrection (Philippians 3:10), so that we can be filled with all the fullness of God.

Both individually and corporately, we are making way for perhaps the last big wave of the Holy Spirit before Jesus returns. God works with us, and we help it to happen.

Healing is God's love for His people, and He has made it available to all who can believe and receive. It is very difficult to serve God effectively while carrying a burden of sickness, whether emotional, psychological, or physical, so He wants to restore and heal in the church, as well as outside. Can we, in turn, extend that love to those who as yet do not know that Christ is alive today?

Nothing is as effective as experiencing God for ourselves. We need to be aware that we are all working for the same side, no matter what denomination or background we have come from. It is not by being Baptists, Anglicans, Methodists, Reformed, or members of any other church that we will make it to heaven, but by being born again. And those who love God must also love one another (John 4:21).

Every large city can have regular outreach meetings. We would like to go on a regular basis to many cities and see how God will demonstrate His healing and saving power there, so dethroning principalities and powers that have reigned in those areas. I believe we all really desire to put action to our words, demonstrating that greater is God that is in us than the devil that is in the world. We have a message worth declaring, that "Jesus Christ is the same yesterday and today and forever." He is always full of mercy and compassion and wants to lift the misery out of people's lives. His promises are sure: He died that we might live; He was whipped and tortured so that we could be made whole. This is the gospel of power unto salvation for healing and for deliverance, and we must proclaim it, expecting God to confirm it with signs following so that we set the whole world talking about God's power.

All of us are aware that time is running out and men's hearts are failing them for fear: fear of violence, fear of unemployment, fears of terrorist attacks, fears about the future, and fears of nuclear war. Many die prematurely of heart attacks and other stress-related diseases. It is very like the days of Noah when men lived for sensual pleasure and were completely uninterested in God. He was not even in their thinking, and as for being saved in an ark – they thought Noah must be mad. "It's never rained before," they said, "it probably won't ever happen." So all perished except Noah and his immediate family. What a tragedy. Yet this is the thinking that is polluting our society today, and I think that we have had enough.

As Christians, we care about our fellow beings, but until recently, we have been so preoccupied with ourselves and with our own fears that we have retreated. I believe God's Spirit is taking hold of us, so that love and concern drive out our fears. This is still a day of God's mercy before the final flood. It is the day of the Lord for evangelism, for communication, for concern, for signs and wonders, and all kinds of functions and ministries in the body of Christ. This is a day prior to the ushering in of the fullness of all things. There will be a fullness of evil, but there will also be a fullness of God's power. The word of God that was first spoken by the prophets is coming to pass, and we can take heart and encourage ourselves in the Lord. For where sin abounds, grace abounds much more. As God says to Habakkuk: "But the Lord is in his holy temple, let all the earth be silent before him" (Habakkuk 2:20). He is on His throne and working His purposes out. There are those of us who have a tendency to view the problems as too big to solve and so retreat, or become completely taken up with the negative spirit of the current crisis to the exclusion of all else. Let us not be guilty of either, but fixing our eyes on Jesus, use our spiritual weapons and the power of the gospel to snatch men from the fire and bring light into the darkness.

Consider the prophetic song of Isaiah (42:13):

*"The Lord will march out like a mighty man, like a warrior he will stir up his zeal; with a shout He will raise the battle cry and will triumph over his enemies."*

He is amongst us as we proclaim our God is alive, our enemies defeated. He has come to set the captives free, and is good news to the poor, the sick and the hopeless. He is life to all who will receive Him. So let us spur one another on and put on the whole armour of God, thinking of others more than ourselves, so that together we can make an impact on those around us, so that the world may know and believe that Jesus lives.

It is a fact that anybody who has had success in any field of work – be it social or creative – has derived their inspiration from somebody else's achievements or personal life. They have been motivated enough for their dreams to become a reality. The Bible says that our young men shall see visions and our old men dream dreams. Take these away from a man or woman and he or she becomes a depressed and unfulfilled person.

Everyone needs a vision from God for his or her own life, family life and ministry. God had a wonderful dream which became a reality. He saw the church – a glorious church – with you and me as vital functioning parts. He saw us as His sons and daughters made in His image, in a love relationship with Him where He is a Father caring and providing and nurturing us into maturity. God's dreams became (and are still becoming) a reality, as the Holy Spirit urges us forward into the glorious vision and possibilities that God has in His mind. He is not only a wonderful creator but He is so convinced of His plans that He has spoken them out and has faith that they will come to fruition through us. He watches over His word to perform it, as He entrusted those first disciples with a commission, a blessing and an anointing to bring His plans to pass. Many more sought the vision and were inspired and empowered by the Holy Spirit to do the works that Jesus did. "The works that I do shall you do also" (John 14:12 [paraphrase]).

We have been greatly influenced by many people in the body of Christ, by their lives and by their gifts and ministries. Many dear people have also encouraged us with love, prayers, and correction, for which we are extremely grateful. It's good to give credit where it's due and so I will mention the names of a few special people who have had particular influence on our lives and ministry.

First, Pastor Sid Purse, who was the pastor at South Chard Fellowship in England, at the time we arrived in need of help in 1968. He introduced us to

Jesus in a new way and always encouraged us to go on when we encountered difficulties, offering us a shoulder to cry on more than once. He inspired us with his love for the Lord and his hatred for the devil. He believed in the Holy Spirit's power to deliver and heal and always sought to bring out God's life and gifts through us. He was never too tired or too busy to spend time on us, no matter what time of day or night we might need him, and that seemed quite often! He lovingly forgot himself and his own needs, moved by his vision that every member of the body of Christ would be functioning in the power of the Holy Spirit, and that we should be witnesses to the fact that Jesus was alive in us. God's love and desires were his one passion, and for that he paid a price. We would never have entered into the ministry without the support of Pastor Purse and his wife, along with many other friends at South Chard.

Having received the Holy Ghost and being keen to get started, we devoured every tape we could about signs, wonders, and the power of the Holy Spirit. Doing the housework, in the bedroom, the bathroom, or the kitchen, everywhere we could plug in the tape recorder, we would listen. I think that tapes must have been stronger in those days to withstand the wear and tear of constant listening! We were fascinated and never tired of the Holy Spirit's ministry, believing that somehow the truth and the anointed word would get into us if we soaked it in long enough.

We heard the American evangelist T.L. Osborne pray for the crippled and deformed whilst holding crusades in Trinidad and Tobago. His messages were so simple and were all taken from the gospel stories of Jesus healing the blind and the lame. You could feel faith rising in the crowds as he spoke, and his voice wasn't a great macho voice but rather the reverse. He utterly believed in the simplicity of the gospel of Jesus Christ, that it is the power of God to salvation to them that believe, and the Word did the work. Thousands were saved, the demonically oppressed were loosed, and the sick healed. God was doing the healing and T.L. preached the gospel message. The delivery was simple, but he seemed to be utterly one with the words he spoke. We also studied his book, The Healing Christ, which simply opened up the Word of God to us and revealed that it was God's will that we should be free of all sickness and pain because Jesus had "borne" them for us.

We also came in contact with Rev. Morris Cerullo, an American evangelist who revealed another dimension of God's work, who showed us how to release the power of the Holy Spirit in praying for others. Sometimes during his meetings in London, England, he had to be carried onto the platform. So great was the anointing of God upon him at that time! As you can imagine, a great reverence for God would come upon the people and many lives were changed and miracles happened. He brought the convicting power of the Holy Spirit in his meetings and the call to men and women to serve God and put their lives in order. The Holy Spirit moved on us many times to go forward and respond to God's will in our lives, receiving a fresh anointing of the Holy Spirit.

One of his favourite messages was taken from John's Gospel: "What shall we do, that we might work the works of God? ...Believe on Him whom He hath sent" (John 6, verses 28-29). We listened to that message hundreds of times, eager to squeeze every drop of revelation from it, and not wanting to miss anything that would fill us with faith and help us to see more clearly. His messages were never very long – at times, quite repetitious – but they brought with them a sense of reverence for God and were always followed by deliverances and healing.

During the '50s there were a number of men moving mightily in healing and deliverance, and one man in particular influenced our lives through his tapes. Jack Coe, a Pentecostal preacher, was considered to be a rather uneducated and even crude preacher, but he had a profound effect on us when we listened to tapes of his ministry in a tent meeting in Washington D.C. For the first time we heard miracles take place. He called out a lady who had her voice box removed, and as he asked God to bring back her voice, she began to speak, first in a whisper and then more clearly: "Praise the Lord, I love you Jesus." It was beautiful. God had performed a miracle and, as you can imagine, there was not a dry eye in the place, and not at home where we were listening to the tape! Jesus was really alive and proving it by performing so many miracles. It created a deep desire in us for the reality of this new life, and so we listened to the tapes over and over until the messages were embedded in our hearts and minds. We knew them almost word for word, and we became motivated to seek God to do the same things.

Another man called William Branham was moving in the gift of the word of knowledge with great power and authority. He used to see the angel of the Lord's presence moving on people in the congregation, and as he did, he would call them out to the front, sometimes sharing their problems and sometimes even giving their names and addresses. He spoke with accuracy, knowing that God had revealed their need and he didn't even have to pray for them. God's knowledge flowing through to people under the anointing of the Holy Spirit is truly wonderful and can bring release to the sick, oppressed, and crushed believer and unbeliever alike.

As you will see later on in this book, Kathryn Kuhlman also left her mark on our lives. We had read a few of her books of healing testimonies but were privileged to attend several of her meetings in the United States, and experience for ourselves the grace and love of God in healing. I say "grace" because when you are in the presence of the Holy Spirit, you forget yourself and your problems and you get caught up with the person of Jesus. That is what Kathryn Kuhlman conveyed to the sick, helpless and dying. She was just a channel for the Holy Spirit to use for His glory, and without that anointing of His presence she was helpless. We were filled with awe as she followed the Holy Spirit, calling out the various illnesses from which people were suffering.

They would then rush out to the front and tell everyone what God had healed them from whilst they were sitting in their seats! Nobody had touched them, only Jesus. Many people had come from great distances to receive their healing, and such was their expectation, that many were healed on the journey to the meetings, or as they stood outside in the crowd waiting for hours to get into the building. The worship was tremendous: one minute we were laughing, the next we were crying as we watched Miss Kuhlman follow the Holy Spirit and repeat what He told her to say to the sick people. Her whole face and expression was full of wonder for Jesus, like a child coming down on Christmas morning to a tree filled with presents. We know from experience that she was just flesh and blood like each one of us. It was Jesus in His compassion and mercy for the ill and suffering that we saw in her; she was just willing to be used by Him. She so frequently said in her meetings, "Jesus, we want You to be seen not me, and we'll be careful to give You all the praise and all the glory for every healing taking place."

There have been many more people who have influenced our lives and ministry, too numerous to mention, but our grateful thanks go to God for all of them for the inspiration and sacrifices they have made to help others. In a sense, these were men and women who pioneered a vision of the healing message of Christ, often bearing the burden alone. Today is a new day in God's purposes, and He deserves that we all understand that His will is to heal the sick and oppressed as we make ourselves available to Him, to bring release and joy into people's lives. He wants us to push back the kingdom of darkness and bring in the Kingdom of God's dear Son. We pray and believe that as we support one another, and move forward in faith, love, and courage, the Holy Spirit will be poured out, mighty signs and wonders will take place throughout all the world, and many will come into the Kingdom of God acknowledging Jesus Christ as Lord.

This book has a cutting edge. But at the same time, we have tried to be as honest as possible about our own experiences – the failures as well as the successes – and to share something of our spiritual journey. The book has a blend of personalities – it is the fruit not only of our own lives, but of some of the lives we have shared in over the years. Should you recognize yourself in any of the illustrations, we trust that none of you will be offended; rather, we hope that you will rejoice to know that your story can be the means to help someone else.

We believe more and more that God wants to move in a powerful way through every member of His church and He draws us together as a team to fulfil His call to "Go ye." Let us take up the challenge and fix our eyes on Jesus, the perfecter of our faith, sharing freely with all men and women the good news that Jesus not only saves from sin but also heals our bodies. Surely He carried the load of our sickness in His own body and with the wounds He bore, we were healed (Isaiah 53). Jesus was the substitute for our pains and sickness, and we can't resist shouting, "Hallelujah, what a Saviour!"

None of us have arrived, and most of us haven't perceived half there is to know on the subject of healing. As we progress in our Christian lives, we find that our perspectives are being changed. That means that what we have written here is in no sense a final statement; even now we are seeing new insights, and we trust that will always be the case. We are learning all the time, but we share with you that which we have seen and heard, so that you can be more fully equipped for this day of God's power.


Rosemary and Ian Andrews

# What is Divine Healing?

It seems to me that there have always been two basic systems of healing: one is man's way and the other is God's. Man's system aims at treating the problem; God's way heals it. When the Lord Jesus came to Earth, He must have done Luke out of a job. Not once did He send anyone to Luke for a pill or a potion. In fact, Jesus might have suggested, "You'd better take up writing, Luke, because your days as doctor are over!"

Now let me say straightaway that I am not against doctors. In thousands of ways, medical science can give relief from pain and sickness for those who do not believe that they can receive it from God. It is God's grace, anyway, which provides the medical knowledge and the miracle of the healing process. (A doctor can set a bone but the actual knitting of the bone is something over which he has no control.) In most cases, there is treatment but not healing, recovery but not full restoration. If you have cancer of the stomach, the doctor can remove half your insides, which may get rid of the problem, but it's not wholeness. If you go to Jesus and He heals you, you still have your stomach and you are completely restored too. If you go to the optician, he can prescribe various lenses for you and cause you to see clearly, but there is no healing there. If you have a bad tooth, the dentist gets the probe and says, "Now this isn't going to hurt very much," (which is usually the first lie you hear) and then he drills out three-quarters of your tooth and fills it up. The toothache is gone, but you are not healed; you've merely had your problem treated. God is merciful in giving us this safety net, BUT HE HAS AN EVEN BETTER WAY. Jesus paid the price to be our doctor. Through His Son, God has committed Himself to making us whole.

When we realize it is God's will to restore and provide for us, when we see the completeness and the certainty of His provision for our health, we stop being filled with fear and doubt, and start expecting to get well. We "enter into rest," as the Bible puts it, and that is the place where we are able to receive all of God's blessings. As long as we are striving, it is difficult for God to get through to us with His gift of healing or any other form of provision, for He rewards faith, not fear.

In our ministry, our whole concept of divine healing is based on this response of faith and love to God's love and faithfulness. This book isn't simply about how to get healed of your sicknesses. It is about how to have a healthy, abundant life through a relationship with God. The teachings on positive confession – on words as a creative force – brought encouragement.

They have been wonderful in bringing a new realization of the believer's authority, the power of the spoken word of faith, and the need for a change of heart in order to allow God's healing to be received. And these are a powerful part of the spiritual weapons that God has entrusted to His people. Jesus said to his disciples that they were to speak to the mountain – that represented their problem – not speak about the mountain; and that if they were to do this and not have doubt in their hearts, then the mountain would be removed and cast into the sea.

I do believe God wants to heal everyone (just as He desires everyone to be saved). He wants us to learn about His provision, His laws, and His unchanging character that He demonstrates in all His dealings with man, so that at least we can put ourselves in a position where we can receive. But much more than just knowledge, God wants us to discover the joy of living in a father-child relationship with Him. Children don't (usually!) demand food, clothing, and shelter from their parents as a legal right, though they have more reason than anyone to expect such care from them. A child's confidence in his mother and father isn't based on his legal standing; he doesn't have to keep threatening his parents with his birth certificate or a phone call to the Child Welfare Services. His confidence flows from the security of knowing that he is loved and his parents want to look after him – and who are committed to doing so. In turn God wants to show us His father heart of love for us. He promises to look after us to the smallest degree, healing us when we become sick, providing for us when we are in need, and listening to us when we cry out. His heart is full of compassion when He sees suffering in any form, yet His ultimate desire is that we receive His life in all its fullness and spend eternity with Him. And a living faith in Jesus is the only cure for the terminal sickness of sin.

This then is what we see as the wonderful uniqueness of God's healing. His grace and our faith mingle in a reciprocal relationship of love to bring wholeness in every part of our being and to sustain us in health. We don't have to keep getting sick and getting healed; God empowers us to share His freedom from pain and disease. It is not a matter of self-effort or knowledge of some theory or philosophy. There are plenty of alternative therapies that may claim to be holistic – bringing a harmony to body, soul, and spirit – and without going into their dangers and deceptions; it often appears they achieve some success. They acknowledge that a physical complaint may have its roots in the mental, emotional, or spiritual realms. But their chief failing is that they cannot minister forgiveness and break the curse that holds all mankind in bondage.

Only divine healing touches every aspect of human life that is under the influence of Satan, bringing:

- forgiveness of sin;
- restoration from sickness;
- freedom from the hold of poverty and adverse social circumstances;
- deliverance from demonic power and influence;
- raising to life for the dead.

More specifically, on an individual level, God is able to restore His image in every area of our life that has been distorted, including our psychological, emotional, intellectual, sexual, social, and spiritual functions. Other forms of healing may claim to offer, for example, peace, enlightenment, self-realization, harmonization of energies, reincarnation, even deification. But only God is able not merely to repair or extend our existing potential, but to fashion a New Creation (2 Corinthians 5:17) within which He Himself dwells by His Holy Spirit.

Some of you may feel to link healing so closely with salvation is taking things too far. Do we need to talk about repentance and sin when we are discussing healing? Is it necessary to receive forgiveness for something before we get rid of our sicknesses? And what has pain and illness to do with Satan? To realize that pain and sickness are essential parts of the curse, which separated man from the state of perfection God gave him in the Garden of Eden, is the starting point of getting healed; and health is at the very heart of the eternal life Jesus won for us when He redeemed mankind on the Cross. This wholeness is what God planned from the moment Adam and Eve stood before Him in guilt and shame, and was promised throughout all the ages until the wonderful fulfilment at Calvary:

> *Surely he took up our infirmities and carried our sorrows, yet we considered him stricken by God, smitten by him, and afflicted. But he was pierced for our transgressions, he was crushed for our iniquities; the punishment that brought us peace was upon him and by his wounds we are healed* (Isaiah 53:4-5).

Our whole attitude will be changed when we realize that pain and suffering, sickness, and disease were never part of God's original plan, and that it was always His intention, after the Fall, to offer those who acknowledged the saving work of His Son the same power over them which Jesus enjoyed.

Instead of passively accepting them as inevitable, or blaming God for His apparent lack of compassion and power, we begin to see we are allowing

Satan to rob us of our inheritance and denying Jesus the ability to give us the full measure of blessing He won for us on the Cross.

Death came into the world through the sin of Adam, and sickness followed in its wake. To the man, God as judge makes it very clear what is the real source of Adam's fear and guilt at facing his Creator. It is not nakedness but disobedience that causes Adam to hide and lie. Though Adam protests that the disaster is all God's fault for giving him a woman who led him astray, God brings the responsibility firmly back to Adam since he had abused God's highest gift of free will in choosing to ignore the command not to eat the forbidden fruit. The curse on Adam resulted in all creation becoming his enemy. Instead of enjoying the fruit of his labours in a world without disease or decay, flood, or drought, he would now have to strive continually to scrape an existence from the hostile land.

> …*Cursed is the ground because of you; through painful toil you will eat of it all the days of your life. It will produce thorns and thistles for you, and you will eat the plants of the field. By the sweat of your brow you will eat your food until you return to the ground, since from it you were taken; for dust you are and to dust you will return (Genesis 3: 17-19).*

Then came the act that must have broken God's heart, for He had to curse not only the man but also the woman. For the woman, what should have been a great joy would become painful. For the rest of time, childbearing, child rearing, and the relationship between husband and wife would be full of stormy conflicts:

> …*I will greatly increase your pains in childbearing; with pain you will give birth to children. Your desire will be for your husband, And he will rule over you (Genesis 3:16).*

To the serpent, God said:

> …*Cursed are you above all the livestock and all the wild animals! You will crawl on your belly and you will eat dust all the days of your life. And I will put enmity between you and the woman, and between your offspring and hers; he will crush your head, and you will strike his heel (Genesis 3:14-15).*

Satan was sentenced to the lowest place on earth for inspiring perpetual conflict between God's people and his own evil offspring. We see both in Scripture and in the ministry today how physical afflictions are often demonically inspired. But we also catch a glimpse of hope: "He will crush your head."

*But when the time had fully come, God sent his Son, born of a woman, born under law, to redeem those under law, that we might receive the full rights of sons (Galatians 4:4-5).*

God Himself in the flesh would provide the sacrifice that would satisfy the claims of justice, and pay the penalty of sin by death. The One who is the very source of existence would throw off the principalities and powers that had wrought havoc in God's world, nailing all our sins and disobedience to a cross. Jesus would be "bruised" as Satan struck back at the real King, taking His rightful position over him. But the triumphant words "He [Jesus] will crush your head" would mean a deadly blow of defeat upon the evil one. Once the head is crushed, there is no more life, and so the serpent's poisonous lies and destructive power would have no more power over us believers.

Here is man's greatest tragedy. For the sake of a fruit, he defied God and exchanged immortality for death, and before death, a life of struggle, toil, and disappointment. In the world today, we see this curse so graphically demonstrated: while one half of the world dies from stress and anxiety, from immorality and self-abuse, the other half starves through the greed and selfishness of the richer nations. Man has lost his way and his only certainty (yet also his greatest dread) is death. Even though our bodies merely return to the dust from which we were made, death still holds a reign of terror over many people, possessing, perhaps, as they do, an inner knowledge that the real sting of death is the eternal separation of the spirit from the source of life which was the true result of Adam's disobedience, *"for the wages of sin is death"* (Romans 6:23).

What a hopeless situation it all seems until we read the rest of the verse from Romans: **"but the gift of God is eternal life in Christ Jesus our Lord."**

Even as God was declaring the inevitable judgment on Adam and Eve which sin demanded in God's perfect world, He was forming His awesome plan for redeeming them. To Adam and Eve, God's act of providing them with garments of skin might have seemed no more than an expression of the love and thoughtfulness He had always shown them. But to us who stand beyond Calvary, we see the mighty significance in God killing an animal to provide for their helplessness. Until this point, blood had not been shed in Eden. But God now provided the first animal sacrifice to show that He Himself would send the blood offering, the covenant sacrifice, which would cover men's sin forever. Adam and Eve's attempts to hide their shame by sewing fig leaves together remind us that our own efforts and religiosity cannot put us right with God; only He can provide the robes of righteousness which symbolize our new life in Christ.

*For if, by the trespass of the one man [Adam], death reigned through that one man, how much more will those who receive God's abundant provision of grace and of the gift of righteousness reign in life through the one man, Jesus Christ (Romans 5:17).*

What a promise! Through the sacrifice of Jesus on the Cross, the curse on Adam is overthrown, and man is restored to his original royal place of rule and authority. No longer sentenced to being a slave, he can be a son! If anyone acknowledges his need and turns to Christ, he will become a child of God and co-heir with Christ of everything in the Father's kingdom:

*And if the Spirit of him who raised Jesus from the dead is living in you, he who raised Christ from the dead will also give life to your mortal bodies through his Spirit who lives in you (Romans 8:11).*

It has always been God's plan to restore to us the blessings of His kingdom. Healing is at the very centre of God's purposes. It is an essential part of salvation. A person healed by God finds, like Job, that he receives twice as much as he had before. Not only does the pain or sickness leave, but also he finds he has renewed strength and joy:

*[He] forgives all your sins and heals all your diseases. [He] redeems your life from the pit and crowns you with love and compassion. [He] satisfies my desires with good things so that your youth is renewed like the eagles (Psalm 103:3-5).*

Even more, compassion and the desire to heal form the very essence of His character. It is an enormous aid to our faith to see how God displays this overflowing faithfulness and love throughout His dealings with mankind. He is a God of integrity and perfection that it would be impossible for Him to withhold blessing and healing from those who earnestly seek Him. Just look at the nature and names of God and see how deeply we can trust Him not only in the area of healing, but also in every area of our lives.

# God the Healer

What is in a *name?* The difficulties parents-to-be have in choosing names for their children reflect the importance we place in a name. Each one has a different connotation and bears a particular meaning. Many of us feel that the name we choose will have an everlasting effect on our child, and it's true that our name can provoke a reaction wherever we go (there must be disadvantages in being called Ann Teake for example, and I once knew a lady called Victoria Station). Writers often use pen names because they are aware their own names don't carry the correct romantic associations. Whenever we want to assert ourselves or promote a sense of authority, we often use our surnames and title or status. In the past, surnames often signified the craft or profession of the bearer, like Carpenter, Butcher, Cutler, Mason, Hedger, and so on. And in the last century names such as Patience, Faith, Mercy, and Constance were very popular, as if parents hoped that by naming their children after these virtues, they would blossom automatically into these temperaments. Names have power. One way or another they are meant to tell us something about a person.

We can trust God. He says I am that I am, there is no moodiness or character flaw to influence the way God deals with His people. The Bible says that God has exulted His Word, above His name. We can know what God will do because it is written in His Word. As I minister throughout the world I frequently find a certain problem even among seemingly mature Christians: many people know a great deal about God, but few really know Him. They have accumulated facts about Him, to which they give mental assent, but often they have never entered into real fellowship with God. Many Christians grow in head knowledge of Scripture but flounder around, unable to overcome habits and receive answers to prayer because they haven't understood the heart of God and the provision He has made to draw us into a unique relationship with Him. This is Paul's urgent prayer for the Ephesians. They already had faith in the Lord Jesus; they had committed their lives to Him and served Him as their Lord, but they still needed to know the Father. This, Paul implies, is not a matter of intellectual study but a spiritual process mediated through our trust in God's grace:

> *For this reason, ever since I heard about your faith in the Lord Jesus and your love for all the saints, I have not stopped giving thanks for you, remembering you in my prayers. I keep asking that the God of our Lord Jesus Christ, the glorious Father, may give you the spirit of wisdom and revelation so that you may know him better. I pray also that the eyes of your heart may be enlightened in order that you may*

*know the hope to which he has called you, the riches of his glorious inheritance in*
*the saints, and his incomparably great power for us who believe...*
*(Ephesians 1:15-19).*

The Apostle Paul repeats this theme in his letter to the Colossians:

*For this reason, since the day we heard about you, we have not stopped praying*
*for you and asking God to fill you with the knowledge of his will through all*
*spiritual wisdom and understanding. And we pray this in order that you may live*
*a life worthy of the Lord and may please him in every way: bearing fruit in every*
*good work, growing in the knowledge of God, being strengthened with all power*
*according to his glorious might... (Colossians 1:9-11).*

It seemed to be of vital importance that people with a newfound faith in
Christ grew in spiritual knowledge of God Himself. This seemed to be the
foundation that would support a life of power and righteousness.

The second reason for exploring the meaning of God's name is to deepen
our understanding of His character is that God says: "For my thoughts
are not your thoughts, neither are my ways your ways" (Isaiah 55:8).
We need to understand and act out His thoughts.

Now usually we assess a person's character by the way he acts and the
things he says. "He's a mean old toad," we complain of someone whose
uncharitable actions have branded him the local Scrooge. On the other
hand, sweet Aunt Alice, who always remembers the children's birthdays and
sends us socks every Christmas, is a "dear old thing who wouldn't hurt a
fly." We judge people by the things they do. Few of us can sum up a person's
character at a glance.

What's more, we expect people to conform to our own standards of
behavior, and we are surprised or shocked by the actions of those who have
a different set of values from our own, however legitimate those values are
to them. This is particularly true in areas such as morality and business. Or
we may think it rude if a person from another culture disregards all our table
etiquette along with his knife and fork and dives into his food with both
hands. Similarly we would be surprised to find, in a Moslem country, that we
had given great offence by showing the soles of our feet!

But if we approach God in the same way, judging His actions and character
by our own human standards of justice and rationality, we can become
bewildered and discouraged. He often works in ways beyond our natural

understanding, for higher purposes than we can perceive, asking us simply to trust Him that, "In all things God works for the good of those who love him" (Romans 8:28). It is far better, then, if we approach God in a different way and interpret all His actions towards us in the light of what we already know about His unfailing love, compassion, and grace.

The Bible is wonderfully geared towards understanding God. Names in Scripture always have a special significance. Many characters receive new names to illustrate God's intervention or divine purpose in their lives: Abraham, Sarah, Peter, and Paul, for example. God Himself is referred to by a number of titles, each one revealing another aspect of His character and the role He promises to fulfil towards His people. In fact, the two are inseparable. Just look at some of the names we find for God in the Old Testament:

Jehovah Sabaoth - - - - - - - - - - the Lord of Hosts
Jehovah Jireh - - - - - - - - - - - - the Lord will provide
Jehovah Rapha - - - - - - - - - - - the Lord that heals
Jehovah Nisi - - - - - - - - - - - - the Lord my banner
Jehovah M'Qaddishkhan - - - - -the Lord that sanctifies

Jehovah Shalom - - - - - - - - - - the Lord sends peace
Jehovah Rohi - - - - - - - - - - - - the Lord my shepherd
Jehovah Tsidkenu - - - - - - - - - the Lord our righteousness
Jehovah Shammah - - - - - - - - the Lord is there

What a God of integrity! Everything He does is an expression of what He is. Blessing overflows from Him like a spring of water. We, who are used to being let down by people and who often fail to keep our word ourselves, find it hard to imagine a God so trustworthy. For in these titles alone, God promises to:

- be our King;
- remove our sicknesses;
- fight for us;
- make us holy;
- give us peace;
- lead and protect us;
- restore our relationship with Him;
- be with us always.

Then, when we take in the other names that are applied to God, we see an overwhelming picture of love, protection and provision. He is God of Salvation, Faithfulness, Mercy, Justice, Comfort, Hope, Love, Life, and Refuge; the Lord is our Rock, our Fortress, our Shield, our Sun, our High Tower, our Deliverer, our Shepherd, our Helper, our Lamp, our Light, our Portion, our Inheritance, our Reward, our Shade, our Redeemer, our Strength and Song, our Resurrection, and our Counsellor. All the power within God is directed towards our blessing. When we see divine healing within this overall context of restoration and provision, sickness begins to lose its hold of fear over us for we see it is part of God's unchangeable nature to make us whole.

In the New Testament, El Shaddai, the God Almighty, reveals Himself as the tender Abba-Father (or more exactly, Daddy) – of His children. This fatherhood of God is the aspect of His nature stressed most strongly by Jesus. He taught His disciples to approach God with the trust and simplicity of a child, encouraging them to address God as Father and to trust in His commitment to care for them:

> *Therefore I tell you, do not worry about life, what you will eat or drink; or about your body, what you will wear. Is not life more important than food, and the body more important than clothes? Look at the birds of the air; they do not sow or reap or store away into barns, and yet your heavenly Father feeds them. Are you not much more valuable than they?... So do not worry saying, "What shall we eat?" or "What shall we drink?" or "What shall we wear?" For the pagans run after all these things, and your heavenly Father knows that you need them. But seek first his kingdom and his righteousness and all these things will be given to you as well (Matthew 6:25-26; 31-33).*

> *Which of you, if his son asks for bread, will give him a stone? Or if he asks for a fish will give him a snake? If you, then, though you are evil, know how to give good gifts to your children, how much more will your Father in Heaven give good gifts to those who ask him! (Matthew 7:9-11).*

Not only does Jesus teach us repeatedly about God's loving character, but also He demonstrates it in His own life, in all His words and actions. His very name – Jesus – means "God saves." He is Emmanuel, living proof that "God is with us." As the Son of God, the Word of God in the form of man, Jesus perfectly expressed the nature of God:

> *In the beginning was the Word, and the Word was with God, and the Word was God He was with God in the beginning...The Word became flesh and made his dwelling among us. We have seen his glory, the glory of the One and Only, who came from the Father, full of grace and truth (John 1:1-2; 14).*

Jesus said:

> "...*Anyone who has seen me has seen the Father*" (John 14:9).

And:

> "*I and the Father are one*" *(John 10:30).*

As the Messiah, the Christ, the Anointed One, He came to do the Father's will and He did only what He saw His Father do. He never suffered any illness or disease. He healed people of sickness wherever He encountered it. He fulfilled the prophecy of Isaiah 61 and set the captives free. His word, His touch brought freedom and wholeness to everyone who sought His help:

> *Great crowds came to him, bringing the lame, the blind, the crippled, the mute, and many others, and laid them at his feet, and he healed them. The people were amazed when they saw the mute speaking, the crippled made well, the lame walking and the blind seeing. And they praised the God of Israel (Matthew 15:30-31).*

Jesus discerned the root of the physical ailment and often declared forgiveness of their sin or commanded them to sin no more. Again and again the Bible records His compassion and love expressed in healing. As John Wimber comments:

> The gospels record forty-one instances of physical and mental healing by Jesus...Of the 3,774 verses in the four gospels, 484 relate specifically to the healing of physical and mental illness and the resurrection of the dead. More impressive, of the 1,257 narrative verses in the gospels, 484 verses – 38.5 percent! – are devoted to describing Jesus' healing miracles... He also equipped the disciples to heal, that they might effectively advance the Kingdom of God. He trained and sent the Twelve and the Seventy-Two (Luke 9: 1-9; 10: 1-24); included healing in the great commission (Mark 16:14-20); and throughout the book of Acts the disciples healed the sick (Power Healing [Hodder & Stoughton, 1986], 58-59).

The wonderful fact that Jesus spent most of His ministry healing the sick and bringing light, hope, and release to those in any form of bondage shows that this is one of God's main concerns. The very heart of God that Jesus reveals is COMPASSION. This is the personal dimension of the loving kindness that was the essence of the Old Covenant. Jesus often healed in response to faith (in fact He always rewarded faith with healing), but He frequently went beyond this to heal because His heart was touched with the feeling of our infirmities. Look at how Jesus responds to the sick when He Himself is full of grief and weariness after hearing of the murder of John the Baptist:

> *When Jesus heard what had happened, he withdrew by boat privately to a solitary place. Hearing of this, the crowds followed him on foot from the towns. When Jesus landed and saw a large crowd, he had compassion on them and healed their sick (Matthew 14:13-14).*

What grace! Overcome with sadness, He did His utmost to escape all the noise and demands of the crowds for a while. How would we have reacted if we had landed at our retreat, worn out with the pain of loss, only to find the deserted beach packed with five thousand crying, desperate, needy people all clamouring for attention? Yet in Jesus there is no trace of anger, resentment or self-pity. With a heart overflowing with love, there is no room for those feelings. Looking away from His own needs, He is moved by the helplessness of the people and heals all their sick. After that, He could legitimately have sent them home, but His compassion extends to the smallest need and He proceeds miraculously to provide food for everyone. Not just a scrap to keep the wolf from the door but a feast, more than they can eat so that there were twelve baskets left over! How can we doubt that God sees our every need and wants to provide for us? We don't have to try and persuade Him to heal us. He hasn't forgotten or overlooked our problems and our sicknesses. All these people did was to be in the right place at the right time and then to ask. They were where Jesus was.

God has always been the same. His nature will never change. Throughout the Scriptures, from Genesis, where we read:

> *God saw all that he had made and it was very good... (Genesis 1:31).*

To Revelation, where John says:

> *Then I saw a new heaven and a new earth...Now the dwelling place of God is with men and he will live with them and be their God. He will wipe away every tear from their eyes. There will be no more death or mourning or crying or pain, for the old order of things has passed away (Revelation 21:1; 3-4).*

God shows there is no deviousness in His character:

> *Every good and perfect gift is from above, coming down from the Father of heavenly lights, who does not change like shifting shadows (James 1:17).*

Creativity, order, beauty, productivity, harmony, and restoration are reflected in all His dealings with mankind, transforming sorrow into joy, suffering into victory, death into life. Knowing His character, we can be confident that these are the fruits that He wants to bring out of every situation, however dark and hopeless it might appear. He cannot fail us, for He cannot act contrary to His nature. We can trust God to keep what we have committed to Him and be free from the burden of fear and anxiety, and have the confidence of David to trust that God desires wholeness in body, soul and spirit:

> *Lord, you have assigned to me my portion and my cup; you have made my lot secure. The boundary lines have fallen for me in pleasant places; surely I have a delightful inheritance. I will praise the Lord, who counsels me; even at night my heart instructs me. I have set the Lord always before me. Because he is at my right hand, I shall not be shaken.*

> *Therefore my heart is glad and my tongue rejoices; my body also will rest secure because you will not abandon me to the grave, nor will you let your Holy One see decay. You have made known to me the path of life; you will fill me with joy in your presence, with eternal pleasures at your right hand (Psalm 16:5-11).*

Remember that when David wrote the passage, he was hiding in the wilderness in fear for his life from Saul. What amazing trust! Was David just a man of great faith as he undoubtedly was, or was there a further reason for his confidence? I think the secret lies in the fact that:

1. He knew the character of God.
2. He knew God personally – he had a relationship with Him.
3. He knew that God was a covenant-keeping God – the God of Abraham and Isaac and Jacob – and David was a beneficiary of the promise made to his forefathers. What was this covenant, this promise, this contract?

# Covenant Terms

It will greatly help our ability to move in faith when we understand that our relationship to God is not based upon a whim but upon an everlasting covenant, and Jesus is our mediator. This New Covenant states:

> *But as surely as God is faithful, our message to you is not "Yes" and "No." For the Son Jesus Christ, who was preached among you by me and Silas and Timothy, was not "Yes" and "No," but in him it has always been "Yes." For no matter how many promises God has made, they are "Yes" in Christ…*
> (2 Corinthians 1:18-20).

We have a categorical promise from God that He will honour Jesus' finished work on the cross.

I have just read that some cars, particularly the Swedish makes, are now sold in Europe with an unlimited guarantee against rust. The promise that the bodywork on your vehicle won't wear out, or if it does, will be mended free of charge, is very tempting; it would be wonderful if we could take out the same guarantee on our own bodywork!

Maybe there is a sense in which we can. We have already seen that God's whole nature and purpose is to restore, make whole and bless. He has done everything necessary for us to live in health and joy and peace. But what is the problem? We often seem unable to appropriate His blessings into our lives. The difficulty lies partly in our understanding the concept of covenant. In our "civilized" society we have lost the knowledge of the contract and the relationship that was interwoven through the whole fabric of the ancient world. When Jesus spoke about making a new covenant, His disciples would have grasped immediately the awe-inspiring implications of what He was doing.

For the most basic sense of covenant is life-long commitment. It means that all I am and all that I have is yours forever. The idea of absolute loyalty and devotion is unfamiliar in our sophisticated Western society; the more civilized we are, the more disloyal we become. The Arabs have a saying: "Blood is thicker than milk" In other words, blood covenant brothers are closer than in a natural family relationship. Our culture reverses that principle.

In the ancient world, a covenant was generally an agreement forged between two tribes. Each of them picked a representative who embodied the qualities, abilities, and characteristics of everyone else in the tribe. Each representative would take off his coat and give it to the other. This symbolized "all that I am I give to you." They would then exchange belts, on which hung their swords, daggers, their bows, and purses, representing commitment of their strength to fight on behalf of the other tribe in time of danger, as well as dedication of all their material wealth. After this, a covenant animal – usually a bull – would be killed and then split down the backbone. Then the two representatives would take the walk of covenance through the two walls of blood in a figure eight which signified infinity, an everlasting bond, which they called upon whatever gods they worshipped to witness. Finally, they cut their wrists or thumb and held them together so that their blood would mingle, and they would swear to keep the covenant between them. The scar they would carry to the grave represented the seal of the covenant, the sign to the world that they had made an eternal, irreversible commitment to one another. They have become friends. How shallow our modern interpretation of the word "friends" compared to its profound implications in the ancient world. Not just anyone could be called a friend, for a covenant brother was the friend who "sticks closer than a brother." That is the true significance of Proverbs 18:24. Jesus is a covenant friend, with all that signifies of a deeper bond than natural brotherhood.

After these solemn proceedings, the representatives would share a covenant meal, usually of bread and wine. Sometimes their blood was dripped into the wine as if to say, "I am giving you my very life and I am drinking your life."

The last effect of a covenant in those days was a name change. Tribe Abecame Tribe AB and Tribe B became Tribe BA. Henceforth they would be inseparably identified with one another, with mutual sharing, love, and protection.

There is a particular covenant word which describes this unique relationship that cannot be adequately conveyed in any single English word. The Hebrew word is hesed and once you understand the full implications of the covenant bond, you will see that only this original word sums up all its qualities. The Authorized Version of the Bible translates it as "mercy." The New American Standard calls it "loving kindness." Other words are "love," "compassion," "loyal love," "covenant or bonded love." Only hesed conveys the idea of "all that I am I give to you, all my strength, my possessions, my abilities, my intellect are at your disposal; anyone who raises a hand against you, will have me to reckon with; when you are in any sort of need, I will always come to your aid; I will never fail you or leave you."

There are other outstanding features of hesed:

1. **Hesed** is a choice word; it is not based on feelings but on an act of the will, a promise of unfailing loyalty.

2. It is a submissive love which is willing to yield in order to serve. It is a love which constantly looks for opportunities to bless.

3. **Hesed** is like a parent-love or womb-love; it is ferociously protective and willing to sacrifice everything to defend the loved one.

4. It is a responsible love. You are your brothers' keeper, an activity that is one of joy and not drudgery to you.

> *"Be strong and courageous. Do not be afraid or terrified because of them, for the LORD your God goes with you; he will never leave you nor forsake you....Do not be afraid; do not be discouraged"* (Deuteronomy 31:6; 8).

Plainly, **hesed** does not come from our human nature. Its selfless devotion and commitment are found perfectly only in the character of God Himself, an expression of the agape love which is the essence of the Godhead.

With this deeper understanding of the meaning of covenant, the examples of covenant in Scripture give an exciting new dimension to our relationship with God. Suddenly we realize the potential for joy and power and fulfilment which is at our disposal. Now when we reread the famous story of David and Jonathan's covenant, we perceive the full wonder and grace of what God has done for us:

> *...Jonathan became one in spirit with David, and he loved him as himself...and Jonathan made a covenant with David because he loved him as himself. Jonathan took off the robe he was wearing and gave it to David, along with his tunic and even his sword, his bow and his belt* (1 Samuel 18:1-3).

David and Jonathan were covenant representatives of their families; all their unborn children in every succeeding generation were to come under the blessing of the vows they took. For Jonathan said to David:

> *...May the Lord be with you as he has been with my father. But show me unfailing*

*kindness like that of the Lord as long as I live, so that I may not be killed, and do not ever cut off your kindness from my family – not even when the Lord has cut off every one of David's enemies from the face of the earth…Go in peace for we have sworn friendship with each other in the name of the Lord, saying, "The Lord is witness between you and me, and between your descendants and my descendants forever"…*(1 Samuel 20:13-15; 42).

We have to remember that these words came from the son of a man who hated David and had already sought to kill him. Saul was insanely jealous of David and must have sowed seeds of suspicion and fear amongst his family towards David for years. Despite this, Jonathan bore a love for David far beyond all natural or reasonable ties. When David hid in the desert for fear of his life from Saul's marauding search parties, we read:

*And Saul's son Jonathan went to David at Horesh and helped him to find strength in God. "Don't be afraid," he said, "my father Saul will not lay a hand on you. You will be king over Israel, and I will be second to you. Even my father Saul knows this." The two of them made a covenant before the Lord…*
(1 Samuel 23:16-18).

The story is well known: how David escapes from Saul; after the death of Saul and Jonathan by the Philistines and the murder of Saul's son Ishbosheth, he eventually sits as God's anointed king on the throne of Israel. Time passes and peace returns to Israel. But every day, as David washes in the morning, he notices the scar on his wrist. Each time, he remembers the covenant he made with his beloved friend, Jonathan. The word "remember" is a covenant word. It means "to hold you always in the forefront of my mind." One day, as he remembers again his friend, a surge of love and grief makes him cry out:

*…Is there anyone still left of the house of Saul to whom I can show kindness for Jonathan's sake? (*2 Samuel 9:1).

There is the covenant word again. Hesed! From the scars of David flow the hesed of the covenant. Any living descendant of Jonathan will be entitled freely and undeservedly to all the riches and blessings of David's family; and hiding in a place called Lo Debar (which means "load of nothing"), miserable, terrified, and in despair is Mephibosheth, the son of Jonathan. He has been a cripple since the age of five when his nurse, who panicked and tried to flee when she heard that Mephibosheth's father had been killed, dropped him. Brought up in an atmosphere of suspicion and hatred, Mephibosheth was indoctrinated by his grandfather with the idea that David is his worst enemy, and if he ever falls into David's hands he will surely be killed. When David becomes king, Mephibosheth's life is dominated by the fear that one day David will hunt him out and murder him. No wonder he called himself a "dead dog" (2 Samuel 9:8).

When a number of David's soldiers ride up one morning to the house where he is in hiding, Mephibosheth is desolated. Unable even to walk, he knows he cannot attempt to escape; giving himself up for lost, he allows himself to be taken to the palace without even asking any questions. But instead of being thrown into a dungeon, he is led into a beautiful room, given a luxurious bath, and dressed in fine new clothes. Bewildered and scared he imagines this must be some subtle form of sadism, for his execution must come soon, and sure enough soon comes the command to appear before the king. This is it, he thinks dully, and when he is led into David's presence, he doesn't even see the smile and the outstretched hand, so he throws himself face down on the floor. Then, amazingly, instead of blows, gentle and unbelievable words fall on his ears:

> *"Don't be afraid," David said to him, "for I will surely show you kindness for the sake of your father Jonathan. I will restore to you all the land that belonged to your grandfather Saul, and you will always eat at my table"* (2 Samuel 9:7).

"I will show you kindness." Hesed – the mercy and grace of covenant love. Not because of anything he is or has done, but simply because of a covenant that was made between his father and David, Mephibosheth will now not only inherit all the worldly goods which had once belonged to his grandfather, but he will also be part of the royal family and will share in everything the king possesses. How hard it must have been for Mephibosheth to grasp this incredible truth, that instead of death he was receiving a glorious lifestyle. No longer was he to be a dog or a servant, but he was to reign like a prince. Impossible to understand, until at breakfast the next morning as David eats, Mephibosheth catches sight of the deep scar on David's wrist and realizes that this is not some wonderful dream but the outworking of hesed, the profound, unfailing love of a covenant bond. So Mephibosheth doesn't need to worry whether this might just be a passing whim of David's and tomorrow he might decide he would like to chop off Mephibosheth's head. It doesn't matter that he deserves nothing and, in fact, all his efforts couldn't win any more. Freely he has received every blessing, and goodness and mercy will follow him all the days of his life:

> *And Mephibosheth lived in Jerusalem because he always ate at the king's table...*
> *(2 Samuel 9:13).*

34

Terrific! David could provide for him, give him a royal lifestyle, watch over him, fight for him, protect him. Yet despite all this, the episode still ends on a slightly sad note, for one thing remained. The verse goes on: "and Mephibosheth was crippled in both feet."

David could give him all these blessings, but he couldn't heal him. Mephibosheth had a wonderful material life, but he would always be crippled. Covenant blessings extend only as far as the abilities and possessions of the covenant makers. So what happens when God makes a covenant with man?

In Genesis 12, we find Abram living in the sacred city of Ur, the country that we today call Iraq in the Persian Gulf. This was a city dedicated to the god and goddess of the moon, and every inhabitant was considered to be a sacred servant-priest of those deities. Yet somehow, amid this saturated atmosphere of magic and idolatry, Abram retained his faith in God Almighty, for the Lord said to him:

> *Leave your country, your people and your father's household and go to the land I will show you. I will make you into a great nation and I will bless you; I will make your name great and you will be a blessing. I will bless those who bless you and whoever curses you I will curse: and all peoples on earth will be blessed through you.*

What a promise! Adam walked out of Eden, responsible for the curse that was levied "all people on earth." Here is God revealing His great plan for reversing that curse through Abram. God's promise is threefold:
1. Abram will be given a land.
2. Abram will become a great nation.
3. Through Abram all the families on earth will be blessed.

Abram was, in all probability, really unable to comprehend what God meant at all. First, normally lone men are not given a whole land to possess, particularly when they are foreign exiles. Second, he is seventy-five years old, his wife isn't much younger, and they have no children and no prospect of being able to have any. So, Abram has made a tremendous act of obedience by leaving Ur and showing that he is serving the invisible God. I'm not sure he really had much faith yet that God will fulfil His word.

In fact, just to "help" God, he takes Lot along with him. By adopting his orphan nephew into his family, he is providing himself with a son and heir. He must have gotten rather hot under the collar when his herdsmen and Lot's herdsmen started to quarrel, as it looked as if there might be outright fighting between them. Abram manages to prevent violence, but there is a split between him and Lot, which meant that Abram is really in trouble: he's lost his heir. In despair, he must have questioned how on earth God was going to bring a great nation out of him, so once more, he gives God a hand by making his servant Eliezer his heir. God has to intervene. A promise alone is not going to convince Abram. Only a covenant will persuade him that God is eternally committed to him and will perform all the miracles He has said. So now God initiates the first step of covenant with the exchange. But instead of coat, shield, sword, and belt, He gives Abram Himself. "Don't be afraid, Abram. I am your shield and your very great reward." I AM, God Himself, will be your strength and protection. What grace to offer mere man all that He is and has! Small wonder that Abram is still unable to comprehend the magnitude of God's action. So with great patience, God explains that it will be Abram's own son who will be his heir. Then He takes him outside and says:

> *...Look up at the heavens and count the stars – if indeed you can count them... so shall your offspring be* (Genesis 15:5).

For the first time we read that Abram actually believes the Lord. He takes his eyes off the impossibility of Sarai conceiving and looks to the power of God Almighty. But a moment later, his faith begins to waver again as he tries to come to terms with the next promise – that he will take possession of the land of Canaan. Or perhaps he thinks that if God will give him a sign that he really will possess the land, then he can believe the Lord for the greater miracle that he will have as many descendants as the stars in the sky. Anyway, he dares to ask God for some proof. And God proceeds with the one mighty, awesome act that will put a seal of unfailing certainty on all He has promised:

> *So the Lord said to him, "Bring me a heifer, a goat, and a ram, each three years old, along with a dove and a young pigeon"* (Genesis 15:9).

God didn't exactly spell it out, but Abram must have been realizing now with growing excitement that he is being told to prepare a **blood covenant sacrifice**:

> *Abram brought all these to him, cut them in two, and arranged the halves opposite each other; the birds, however, he did not cut in half* (Genesis 15:10).

Just as everything is ready, the precious sacrifice is almost stolen, birds of prey come down on the carcasses and Abram has to drive them away. I believe many things can try and rob us of God's provision – doubt, fear, the devil. We need to exercise our own faith and strength of will in times of challenge. Then we read:

> *As the sun was setting, Abram fell into a deep sleep, and a thick and dreadful darkness came over him.*

One of the joys of the blood covenant relationship with God is that we can enter into rest. We can cease from our own works when we realize that God makes available to us His ability and power. He put Abram to sleep because there was absolutely nothing that Abram could contribute in a covenant with the Lord God Almighty. What could he give God? All that he had came from God – his health, his wealth, his strength. So God made him fall asleep and then,

> *When the sun had set and darkness had fallen, a scorching firepot with a blazing torch appeared and passed between the pieces.*

We have already learned that in a blood covenant, the two representatives walked in a figure eight through the pieces of the sacrifice, between a wall of blood. So here we witness the amazing miracle of Jesus (the blazing torch) making a covenant with His Father on Abram's behalf, the Light of World walking through the pieces and,

> *On that day the Lord made a covenant with Abram and said "To your descendants I give this land…" (Genesis 15:18).*

But, as yet, God still does not finish the covenant. They have not yet shared the covenant meal together. For God can see that Abram has still not come to the point of covenant faith which means total commitment to God. He still cannot just receive what God has promised. He still tries to offer God something. So despite this wonderful sign, Abram still cannot leave the problem of having a child up to God.

I shouldn't think Sarai was much encouragement. She hadn't been in on any of these talks with the Lord and she probably thought Abram's ramble about having a baby was senile decay or the product of too much sun. After ten years of nothing happening, Abram began to wonder if she wasn't right, so when she suggested he try to have a child by her servant Hagar, he gave in and slept with her. Thus Ishmael was born, and Abram was thrilled. At last, at last, he had an heir. Now God's promise could be fulfilled. But how sad. Abram thought he could help God, but he was way off the mark, and he was only delaying God's blessing. How can you fault a person who is trying to fulfil God's purpose, though? Satan is so subtle. The whole idea of covenant with God is supernatural, however, and there is nothing man can do to bring it to pass.

For thirteen years, Ishmael was brought up as Abram's son and heir, shown every honour and showered with love. Then just as he was at the point of entering manhood, God yet again appeared to his father and repeated His original promise. But this time He revealed more of His plan and character to Abram, and by the way He spoke, made it clearer that there was a new covenant relationship between them:

> ...I am God Almighty; walk before me and be blameless. I will confirm my covenant between me and you, and will greatly increase your numbers...You will be the father of many nations. No longer will you be called Abram; your name will be Abraham for I have made you a father of many nations (Genesis 17:1-5).

Here is another mark of covenant – an exchange of names. The very essence of God's name, the sound in the centre of Yahweh, which no one knew exactly how to pronounce but which was almost like a breath, was incorporated in Abram's name. And henceforth God deigned to be called the God of Abraham. This incredible blessing is conveyed to Abraham's wife too:

> ...As for Sarai your wife, you are no longer to call her Sarai; her name will be Sarah. I will bless her and will surely give you a son by her. I will bless her so that she will be the mother of nations; kings of peoples will come from her (Genesis 17:15-16).

And Abraham falls on the floor, laughing. Even after all that has happened he still can't see beyond his human limitations. He thinks that through Ishmael, the promises of God can come true without having to resort to the supernatural (or the ridiculous!). God can't be serious. He must mean Ishmael:

> "If only Ishmael might live under your blessing!"

"Yes," says God, "but I have an even higher plan":

> "Your wife Sarah will bear you a son and you will call him Isaac" [which means "he laughs," or more exactly in Hebrew, "hahaha"!]

It is almost as if God is laughing with Abraham, for in the womb of human helplessness, God has formed His answer for mankind. This is the hilarity of true faith when we come into the joy of abandonment to God, beyond struggle, beyond reason, beyond hope, into faith. And now the covenant is almost finalized, for Abraham is circumcised, taking upon himself and on every member of his family the sign of his remarkable agreement with God.

So now Abraham, now ninety-nine years old, is by faith, expecting a son within the year. But there remains one problem. Sarah is, after all, barren. Always has been, and she is an old woman. God hasn't given her any of these wonderful promises. She only has Abraham's word to go on. There's only one thing for it: she has to hear the Lord Himself say these things.

A few days later, Abraham is resting at the entrance of his tent in the middle of the day when he sees three men approaching. Hospitality is very important in his culture, and Abraham begs the men to stay while he hastily orders a delicious meal. While they eat, Abraham stands a little way off, watching them discreetly from the shade of a tree. They look like ordinary men, but with the eyes of his growing faith, Abraham begins to realize that one of them is the Lord. For as he sees one of them break the bread and hold some out to him, the glorious fact dawns on him that this is his covenant Lord sharing the covenant meal, the meal that signifies: It Is done. Sure enough, when his ears hear the wonderful promise repeated once more, Abraham is convinced that this is indeed El Shaddai, the Lord God Almighty:

> ... *"I will surely return to you about this time next year, and Sarah your wife will have a son" (Genesis 18:10).*

Suddenly from behind the curtain of the tent there is a great explosion of laughter. Sarah has been eavesdropping on the conversation, and the thought of her having a baby at her age with a husband who is nearly a hundred years old has her doubled up with mirth. The Lord can read her thoughts perfectly, but instead of being angry at her unbelief, He makes allowances for the limitations of human understanding and reassures them:

> *Is anything too hard for the Lord? I will return to you at the appointed time next year and Sarah will have a son (Genesis 18:14).*

And now – at last – Abraham has entered into covenant faith.

God Himself has fulfilled all the terms of the covenant, and Abraham recognizes that he is now a covenant beneficiary. He has come to the end of all his own ideas and ability. It is now completely up to God and Abraham has confidence that God will perform what He promised. As far as his eyes can see and his mind can understand, situation is still hopeless but now it doesn't bother him. Even when Abimelech accidentally takes Sarah as a wife (remarkable when you consider she is almost ninety!), Abraham still believes that God can fulfil His promise. So we read:

> *By faith Abraham, even though he was past age – and Sarah herself was barren – was enabled to become a father because he considered him faithful who had made the promise (Hebrews 11:11).*

The text is ambiguous here, and this verse could refer to Sarah. Anyway, both of them were now completely committed to God's way of doing things, and this faith gave them the physical ability to conceive a child. This was not virgin birth. Isaac was the natural, yet supernatural, child from their own bodies:

> *Against all hope, Abraham in hope believed and so became the father of many nations, just as it had been said to him, "So shall your off- spring be." Without weakening in his faith, he faced the fact that his body was as good as dead – since he was about a hundred years old- and that Sarah's womb was also dead. Yet he did not waver through unbelief regarding the promise of God, but was strengthened in his faith and gave glory to God, being fully persuaded that God had power to do what he had promised. This is why "it was credited to him as righteousness" (Romans 4:18-22).*

After all his doubts, it was the covenant which gave Abraham the strength to believe God. He now had not only a promise but also an oath:

> *Because God wanted to make the unchanging nature of his purpose very clear to the heirs of what was promised…God did this so that, by two unchangeable things in which it is impossible for God to lie, we who have fled to take hold of the hope offered to us may be greatly encouraged (Hebrews 6:17-18).*

Having entered into covenant with God, Abraham was able to face everything in his situation that should have made him give up, and actually praise God. As he gave glory to God, his faith grew even stronger. He was as pregnant with faith as Sarah was with child, and at the appointed time the vindication of his faith was revealed to the world:

> *Now the Lord was gracious to Sarah as he had said, and the Lord did for Sarah*

*what he had promised. Sarah became pregnant and bore a son to Abraham in his old age, at the very time God had promised him (Genesis 21:1-2).*

It is Sarah who sums up the real reward of this long trial of faith.

*…God has brought me laughter, and everyone who hears about this will laugh with me (Genesis 21:6).*

Fulfilment of the promise is always the outcome of faith. It is the fruit of clinging to the Lord's promises, of trusting in the faithfulness of our covenant God who promises to give us all that He is and has. God is a miracle worker and He wants to work on our behalf.

Before we leave the story of Abraham, we should note that it reveals one important lesson for us. God had become everything to Abraham. All possibilities for life and peace lay in El Shaddai (the God who is more than enough). God had revealed to Abraham His very nature, and Abraham had come to put his trust in that faithfulness and love, and not in the miracle he hoped for. How else could Abraham have gone through the incredible test of being told to sacrifice Isaac, his miraculous son of promise? After years of waiting, the impossible had happened; Abraham might have thought he had reached his goal of faith.

But God asked him to go one more step. And if you are mature in your faith, God might well ask you to do the same. After going through years of refining and discipleship, God leads you into a wonderful ministry of preaching, or teaching or healing – only to tell you to give it up, to lay it on the altar as a burnt offering. Without covenant faith, you may fight for your ministry. But if you have trust in the perfect love of your covenant God you will know that whatever He asks will be for your good, and you will be prepared to lay down the thing you most treasure in order to receive God's best for you. He may well give it back to you at the last minute as He did with Abraham, but the important thing is being prepared to lose, to die, in order to gain Christ.

In this part of the story, Abraham was entering a new dimension in covenant relationship with God. Hitherto he had been told to believe a promise that could only bring him joy; now he was being asked to destroy the very fulfilment of that promise with no explanation or reassurance. Abraham's amazing prompt, unquestioning obedience reflects the fact that his long years of waiting have so refined his faith that now he really does know his God. Before God even reveals another of his covenant names, "The Lord

Your Provider," Abraham has confidence that the Lord will again perform some miracle. This is why he calls this terrible act of killing Isaac **worship.**

> *"Stay here with the donkey," he said to his servants, "while I, and the boy, go over there. We will worship, and then we will come back to you."*

Abraham is so convinced of the loving kindness of the Lord that he is sure that somehow he will return with his beloved son. Even if he had to go through with the sacrifice, Abraham believes that God can raise Isaac from the dead because God has promised that through this son all the nations of the world will be blessed. And God cannot lie. So when Isaac asks

> *"The fire and wood are here, but where is the lamb for the burnt offering?"*
>
> *Abraham replies, "God himself will provide the lamb for the burnt offering, my son."*

Yet he still has to get to the point of lifting his knife to slay Isaac, before the angel of the Lord stops him:

> *"Do not lay a hand on the boy...Do not do anything to him. Now I know that you fear God, because you have not withheld from me your son, your only son." Abraham looked up and there in a thicket he saw a ram caught by its horns. He went over and took the ram and sacrificed it as a burnt offering instead of his son. So Abraham called that place The LORD Will Provide...*
> (Genesis 22:12-14).

So we can reach that point of total abandonment to God, of utter commitment to HIM over and above all other hopes and desires. For it is in that realm of true worship, when we lay down our life on the altar that God is able to provide for all our needs. Let us look in more detail at how, in our helplessness, God is our strength, and how, ultimately, God has provided an even better covenant of life and blessing based not on law, but on grace.

# Covenant Provision and a New Covenant

*...The Israelites groaned in their slavery and cried out, and their cry for help because of their slavery went up to God. God heard their groaning – and he remembered his covenant with Abraham, with Isaac and with Jacob. So God looked on the Israelites and was concerned about them* (Exodus 2:23-25).

Here we find the seed of the miracle that took place on the night of the Passover. God remembered His covenant with Abraham. All that He planned to bless Abraham's descendants with was brought forcibly to His mind, and He prepared the remarkable plan that would set them free. The first thing He did was to call Moses from the burning bush and appoint him as His covenant representative. Moses was convinced He had the wrong man. To be fair, anyone else would have thought that too. He might have been brave enough, in the heat of the moment, to kill the Egyptian beating a fellow Hebrew, but as far as being a leader and a spokesman was concerned,
he was just a joke. Not only was he meek and timid, but there is every possibility he actually had a speech defect:

> *Moses said to the LORD, "O Lord, I have never been eloquent neither in the past nor since you have spoken to your servant. I am slow of speech and tongue"* (Exodus 4:10).

But all these inadequacies are irrelevant when God has given him His covenant promise that He will bring the Israelites out of Egypt into a land flowing with milk and honey. Not only that, but God's oath is sealed by His own name, by which God assures Moses that all that I AM will be given to His people, for He is committed to them forever:

> *God said to Moses, "I am who I am. This is what you are to say to the Israelites: 'I AM has sent me to you.'" God also said to Moses, "Say to the Israelites, 'The Lord, the God of your fathers – the God of Abraham, the God of Isaac and the God of Jacob – has sent me to you.' This is my name for ever, the name by which I am to be remembered from generation to generation"* (Exodus 3:14-15).

The Hebrew for "Lord" sounds like and may be derived from the Hebrew for "I AM." Up till now, God has been known as El Shaddai, God Almighty; with the forging of the covenant, God has made possible a more personal relationship with His people, and by revealing this name **I AM** WHO I AM, or THE LORD, He promises to carry out all He has said He will do, because He is a God of integrity and faithfulness. In other words, He is showing them that He loves them. By revealing to them this name, God is trying to quicken the Israelites' faith and revive their memory of the covenant He has made with them. Humanly, their situation is hopeless, but if they can recall the covenant, they can lift up their heads and look towards the promised land. He even repeats this new name by which He will be known to them and gives them through Moses a further promise of deliverance:

> **...I am the Lord.** *I appeared to Abraham, to Isaac and to Jacob as God Almighty, but by my name the Lord I did not make myself known to them. I also established my covenant with them to give them the land of Canaan, where they lived as aliens. Moreover, I have heard the groaning of the Israelites, whom the Egyptians are enslaving, and I have remembered my covenant.*
>
> *Therefore, say to the Israelites:* **'I am the Lord,** *and I will bring you out from under the yoke of the Egyptians. I will free you from being slaves to them, and I will redeem you with an outstretched arm and with mighty acts of judgment. I will take you as my own people, and I will be your God. Then you will know that I am the Lord your God, who brought you out from under the yoke of the Egyptians. And I will bring you to the land I swore with uplifted hand to give to Abraham, to Isaac and to Jacob. I will give it to you as a possession. I am the Lord"* (Exodus 6:2-8).

Four times God promises the Israelites that He will be true to His perfect character of righteousness and love. Four times He reassures them that He will not fail them, that He will deliver them and bless them – and not because of a passing whim but on the basis of two unshakable, unchangeable things: His character and His covenant.

How sad that the Israelites are too discouraged and oppressed by their bondage to believe these promises (Exodus 6:9). This is sometimes the case with healing, that even though we come to a sick person with a word of knowledge or the message of God's covenant love and provision, they are too depressed by their pain to believe there is any hope. It is pointless praying for their healing until the root of discouragement and dismay has been dealt with and they have received God's love and the Lordship of Jesus. Because the Israelites couldn't see any other lords except the Egyptians, God kept saying, "I am your Lord," but every moment of their tortuous day, they were reminded that Pharaoh ruled over them. And sometimes our illness can become our lord. It dictates all our thoughts and actions. Everything we do is with reference to our physical condition. But if we reject that domination, or are delivered from that bondage and receive the yoke of Jesus instead, we are able to step outside our problem and share God's perspective that means health and deliverance.

It takes nine plagues, nine incredible demonstrations of God's power, before the Israelites begin to see a genuine glimmer of hope. Only when they are told of the last terrible plague to come upon the Egyptians, the death of all the first-born, and of God's protection over the Israelites, do they realize that, true to His word, God is going to deliver them. Nothing about their circumstances has changed yet, but their hearts have changed. Look at the difference in their response to Moses' command to prepare the Passover meal:

> *...Then the [Israelites] bowed down and worshiped* (Exodus 12:27).

This, then, is the attitude in which they take a lamb and sacrifice it for this remarkable meal. WORSHIP. And when we let go, and fall at the Lord's feet in worship. He is then able to deliver us from bondage. That day, two million slaves prepared a feast for themselves, as if they were kings. It must have really rattled the Egyptians. "What on earth are those crazy Israelites doing now?" The air is filled with the smell of 250,000 lambs roasting on spits! And the Israelites are praying and praising their God. Have they gone mad? If we rejoice in the Lord in the face of our enemies, in the midst of sickness and Satan's bondage, we too will confuse and overthrow the opposition.

When the lambs were slaughtered, the Israelites had been told to dip a bunch of hyssop, a bitter herb symbolizing their bondage, into the blood, and paint the posts and lintel of their doors. Then all the family were to walk through the door and eat every scrap of the meat which had been cooked. Did they do so with a growing, amazed realization that they were partaking in a covenant meal? Perhaps, but Moses certainly knew that all that was happening was the outworking of God's covenant promise, so he may not have been as astounded as the rest of them when they ate the lamb and found themselves healed of every affliction. For they had walked through the walls of blood, just as one would do in a covenant sacrifice. And now they were eating a meal and breaking unleavened bread together, the bread of repentance, and a statement, therefore, that they were leaving behind sin, as if to finalize that covenant. Anyway, what they did was an amazing act of faith, standing eating this meal in their travelling clothes when everything about their situation said that they would be back under the whips of the Egyptians in the morning. But not far away, there were wails of grief and despair as family after Egyptian family discovered the eldest son dead in his bed. God was faithful. That very night Pharaoh ordered the Israelites to go and a few hours later, laden with the gold and silver of the Egyptians, they were on the road to freedom.

And not alone:

> *By day the Lord went ahead of them in a pillar of cloud to guide them on their*
> *way and by night in a pillar of fire to give them light, so that they could travel by*
> *day or night. Neither the pillar of cloud by day nor the pillar of fire by night left*
> *its place in front of the people* (Exodus 13:21-22).

Deliverance had come. All they did was OBEY GOD: they fed on the right
food, which was in a spiritual sense the Lamb of God, the Lord Jesus Christ,
even though they had no idea that this act prefigured the New Passover, the
deliverance that would come to all mankind through the sacrifice of the
Lamb. What is more, we read in Psalm 105:37:

> *He brought out Israel, laden with silver and gold, and from among their tribes* **no**
> **one faltered.**

After years of poverty and ill-treatment, not a single one of the two million
Israelites stumbled or fainted on the way. Weak and undernourished as they
must have been before that Passover Meal, now they were supernaturally
restored and empowered with the strength for this epic escape in the face
of huge dangers and obstacles. What a remarkable thing, and what an
encouragement to us to see the life and restoration available in the blood of
Jesus, the New Passover Lamb.

Very soon, however, the Israelites encountered their first trial of faith.
They were overjoyed they had been delivered from the Egyptians, but what
had they been delivered into? We read that they wandered round the land
in confusion, hemmed in by the desert (Exodus 14:3) and then suddenly,
they looked up and saw the entire Egyptian army with horses, troops, and
chariots marching after them. And they couldn't escape for in front of them
was the impenetrable barrier of the Red Sea. After the wonderful proof
they had of God's power and love, what did they do? Panic.

> *...They were terrified and cried out to the Lord. They said to Moses, "Was it*
> *because there were no graves in Egypt that you have brought us to the desert*
> *to die? What have you done to us by bringing us out of Egypt? Didn't we say to*
> *you in Egypt, 'Leave us alone; let us serve the Egyptians'? It would have been*
> *better for us to serve the Egyptians than to die in the desert!"*
> (Exodus 14:10-12).

We may have this experience in healing – that after the first deliverance or touch, the problem comes back with a vengeance. This may be due to one or two factors, which we will discuss in the section on "How to pray for the sick," but it is worthwhile just noting here what Moses' reply was in this situation:

> ...*Do not be afraid. Stand firm and you will see the deliverance the Lord will bring you today. The Egyptians you see today you will never see again. The Lord will fight for you; you need only to be still* (Exodus 14:13-14).

Whatever the cause of the return of the problem, it is no good fretting and striving. We need to stand firm in our faith, be still, and see the Lord accomplish the deliverance. Fear will stop us seeing beyond our problem. But if we look to the Lord, the Red Sea of our difficulties or sickness will open up before us and we will cross over safely.

At last everything was going well for the Israelites. The Egyptian army was all drowned and they had a marvellous time of rejoicing on the shore of the Red Sea, singing, dancing and praising God for their wonderful deliverance. It didn't look as if they could ever doubt God again. But only three days later they found themselves in the wilderness, wandering around in the heat and dust without water. And when they eventually did find water at Marah, it was undrinkable.

This is another trial of faith that are sent to develop our faith, not to destroy it; to deepen our trust in God, not to undermine it. But this doesn't happen automatically. Only if we look to the Lord will our faith grow stronger. And that requires a conscious and sustained effort. It means denying your senses, your feelings, and your reason. But if we look at our problem, it gets bigger and bigger until it finally overwhelms us. We can't see anything except how hopeless everything is. So we have to be ruthless with ourselves and give not only our problem, but our very selves, over to the Lord for His answer.

God does not tell us to look at our mountains of testing but to speak to them!

God was testing the Israelites. Now testing implies trying out the quality and strength of something and God wanted to discover what was in the hearts of the people. At least, He knew very well what was in their thoughts, but they themselves didn't know. Very often, difficulties draw out what is hidden inside us, the bad as well as the good, just as refining of gold and silver require them to be heated until all the impurities rise to the surface and can be scooped off. With the Israelites, after years of slavery, when they had little freedom of choice, no rights, and were totally dependent on the Egyptians, they had to learn that they must look somewhere else to meet all their needs. (There is, after all, a certain security in bondage. This is why some people ultimately prefer their sicknesses to the responsibility of health). God wanted to teach them to rely wholly on Him. Now that they were no longer forced to serve a ruler and work for hard taskmasters, He longed for them to choose to obey Him out of love. Even at this stage, God was seeking an intimate relationship with His people rather than a rule of law. Already He was demonstrating that He wanted to be a father to them. This purpose is seen clearly in Deuteronomy 8 as they finally near the promised land:

> *Remember how the Lord your God led you all the way in the desert these forty years, to humble you and to test you in order to know what was in your heart, whether or not you would keep his commands. He humbled you, causing you to know hunger and then feeding you with manna, which neither you nor your fathers had known, to teach you that man does not live on bread alone but on every word that comes from the mouth of the Lord. Your clothes did not wear out and your feet did not swell these forty years. Know then in your heart that as a man disciplines his son, so the Lord your God disciplines you* (Deuteronomy 8:2-5).

God knew that they would be full of enthusiasm for serving Him as long as He was rolling back the waves of the Red Sea and drowning their enemies, but would they trust Him and love Him when things weren't going so well, when God's help seemed to be absent? Would they demonstrate covenant faith or human faithlessness? And would a "proud and stiff-necked people" allow God both to reign over them and provide for them (for it can sometimes be as hard to be served as to submit)? Or would they want to go their own way, now that they were free from domination?

Unfortunately, the Israelites had short memories. Unlike God who constantly "remembered" His covenant with that faculty of covenant faithfulness and commitment, they turned their back on Him at the first hurdle. They began to mutter and complain as moment by moment they felt their tongues swell. Then as they looked around and saw nothing but rock, sand and more sand for miles, they really began to panic. You can just imagine it:

"We're all going to die in this God-forsaken wilderness. What was the point of escaping from Egypt just to rot here in this desert? We must have been mad to trust Moses. We always thought he was a bit stupid and now he's proved it."

If the people of Israel thought they had a problem, Moses' problem was about two million times more. After all, he was responsible for the whole tribe. They had followed his lead, and in this time of crisis, he had to find the faith to hold on to God's promise, and bring His divine provision to the people. Moses had a choice. He could either stare at the undrinkable water and feel hope ebb away like the tide, or he could look to the One who gives living water, the Lord God. Glancing at the people wailing around the pool, Moses knew that soon he was going to have a riot on his hands. So what did he do? He lifted up his head and cried out to the Lord. He didn't waste time trying to dig holes to find water. He just threw himself upon His covenant Lord and gave God the problem of saving them all from dying of thirst. For God's covenant promise was that when they were in trouble, He would deliver them. How He would do it was God's responsibility. Moses' trust was in Him and His faithfulness, not in the answer. And because he let go of his problem, God was able to release that answer to Moses, just as a drowning man can only be saved when he stops clutching and grabbing, and trusts in his rescuer.

> *Then Moses cried out to the Lord. ...And the Lord showed him a [tree]...*
> *(Exodus 15:25).*

What sort of an answer was that? A fork of lightning flashing into the pool would have been a bit more convincing, and certainly more impressive. But quite often the Lord's provision doesn't look like a very good idea at all from our point of view. Sometimes it seems far too simple; or else God asks us to do something that seems quite unrelated to our immediate problem. Look at the story of the blind man Jesus told to go and wash in the Pool of Siloam. But God is sometimes testing us to see whether we will be obedient, and we will only obey if our heart is full of love and trust and we are prepared to exercise our faith. Moses could have felt he was going to lose all remaining credibility in the eyes of the Israelites; and God wanted to see what mattered most to him - the praise of the people, their good opinion, or favour with God by doing His will. Where were his eyes – on the people or on the Lord? Fortunately for them all, Moses didn't waver. He had asked God for help and he believed that the tree was His provision so he threw it right into the heart of the problem. Picking up the piece of wood, he hurled it into the water:

*And the water became sweet.*

So often, we have to take the first step and God confirms. In the New Testament we read that God confirmed His word with signs and wonders, so the disciples evidently had to preach and act on their faith first and then God did the rest. There are many instances where people had to actually rise up and walk first before they knew they were healed, and then often would come the verbal confirmation that their faith had made them whole. So here, Moses acted in faith, received the miracle and then God confirmed it again with a promise. For there at Marah, God covenanted to be their Healer. He had proved to them He could do it, and now He committed Himself to being their health. He revealed to them the wonderful fact that His very nature generates the gift of healing and strength. For He tells them of yet another name by which He may now be known: Jehovah Rapha – the Lord your healer.

> *…There the Lord made a decree and a law for them, and there He tested them. He said, "If you listen carefully to the voice of the Lord your God and do what is right in his eyes, if you pay attention to his commands and keep all his decrees, I will not bring on you any of the diseases I brought on the Egyptians for* **I am the Lord, who heals you**" (Exodus 15:25-26 [emphasis added]).

Notice, though, that the Lord's promise of healing here was conditional. He didn't say I love you so much that whenever you get sick, I will heal you immediately. Of course, this was God's provision under the law, before the grace of the New Covenant had come; but still, it shows God's desire for wholeness, for spiritual and moral health, rather than physical well being alone. In fact, some people do discover that being well in itself is of little good if they are without peace, without joy, and without hope in the world.

We see then that the basic principle God lays down here is that their healing is conditional upon their obedience to His laws and His ways, that health is the reward of righteousness, and throughout the Old Testament we see God blesses those who keep His commands. It does not always follow, though, that those who sin automatically get sick, and it is a question often raised in the Old Testament – why do the righteous sometimes suffer while the wicked prosper? Psalm 73 puts this into God's eternal perspective, and concludes that, ultimately, the wicked do perish, and even in this life their comfort is often short-lived. But still, our own experience tells us that on many occasions we find God healing non-Christians who may or may not subsequently turn to Him, or sometimes even healing people who are living blatantly immoral or disobedient lives, who even while reaching out to God on a strand of faith, do not necessarily have any intention of changing their ways, and who, even in the light of God's manifest power and love, may subsequently refuse to turn and thank Him. Such is God's mercy. As we have seen, the very essence of God's character is to heal and restore, and these gifts overflow from Him. With the redeeming sacrifice of Jesus and the establishment of the New Covenant, such a river of divine love and grace flooded over mankind that some people get healed simply by "being in the way," with their tiny portion of faith. And repeatedly through the history of the Israelites in the wilderness we find God having mercy on them and healing them despite their continued doubt and disobedience. Usually, though there was faith somewhere, which God honoured on behalf of the rest of the nation, or there was a measure of repentance:

• Further on in the desert, the people of Israel thought they would die of hunger and railed at God for abandoning them – He replied by sending manna and quails to sustain them.
Exodus 16

• Their rebellion against God grew so great that He sent a plague to destroy them – but the faith of Moses and Aaron stopped His anger and brought the plague to an end.
Numbers 16

• Miriam was smitten with leprosy for speaking against Moses – but God healed her when Moses pleaded on her behalf.
Numbers 12

• Despite the lessons of Marah, the Israelites thought they would once more die of thirst in the wilderness of Zin and raised another cry of self pity and reproach – and God provided for them when Moses struck the rock with his rod and released the water of Meribah.
Numbers 20

• They complained again about how much better off they would have been in Egypt and so God sent a plague of fiery red serpents among them – but when they repented, God told Moses to set a bronze snake on a pole and anyone who looked at it would be healed.
Numbers 21

Never in the history of mankind has there been a record of such consistent faithlessness on Israel's side and such overwhelming love and faithfulness from God. In these examples, we see how the full grace of the New Covenant, reflected in the awesome sacrifice of God's only Son, is foreshadowed in the Old. Blessing and restoration, then, are promised to all who keep God's laws:

*If you pay attention to these laws and are careful to follow them, then the Lord your God will keep his covenant of love with you, as he swore to your forefathers. He will love you and bless you and increase your numbers. He will bless the fruit of your womb, the crops of your land – your grain, new wine and oil – the calves of your herds and the lambs of your flocks in the land that he swore to your forefathers to give you. You will be blessed more than any other people; none of your men or women will be childless, nor any of your livestock without young. The Lord will keep you free from every disease. He will not inflict on you the horrible diseases you knew in Egypt, but He will inflict them on all who hate you*
(Deuteronomy 7:12-15).

Wonderful promises to the Israelites! So how much more can we expect who live under the New Covenant? God never contradicts Himself and His eternal purpose is always the same. But what has changed is that the New Covenant has made it possible for our hearts to be changed, for the righteousness of God, which is Jesus, to dwell inside us so that we live lives pleasing to God, for "We have been made holy through the sacrifice of the body of Jesus Christ once for all" (Hebrews 10:10).

This amazing new relationship with God, based not on law but on love, is prophesied by Jeremiah:

*"The time is coming," declares the Lord, "when I will make a new covenant with the house of Israel and with the house of Judah. It will not be like the covenant I made with their forefathers when I took them by the hand out of Egypt because they broke my covenant, though I was a husband to them," declares the Lord. "This is the covenant that I will make with the house of Israel after that time," declares the Lord.* **"I will put my law in their minds and write it on their hearts. I will be their God and they will be my people.** *No longer will a man teach his neighbour or a man his brother, saying, 'Know the Lord,' because they will all know me, from the least to the greatest," declares the Lord. "For I will forgive their wickedness and remember their sins no more"* (Jeremiah 31:31-34 [emphasis added]).

### These are the terms of the New Covenant:

1. God's laws will be in our hearts.

2. We will be a "peculiar" people, a people set apart for God.

3. We will know God personally.

4. Our sins will be forgiven and forgotten.

5. He will be our Provider and Healer.

In the light of what we now understand about covenant, let us look briefly at the way in which this New Covenant was made.

First, a covenant representative was required. As with Abraham, no ordinary man could make a covenant with God because he had nothing to offer an almighty, perfect God. What was needed was someone at once completely human yet also completely sinless.

Since no one could be without sin except God Himself, the representative had to partake of the divine nature. As the Son of God, Jesus fulfilled all the requirements of the covenant. Sometimes we are so intent on proving Christ's deity that we forget He is also a man. We have only to see the importance laid on Christ's genealogy in the Gospels to realize that the disciples saw Him as truly one of them, not a visitor from outer space. He was born of Mary and took on our humanity. Made of flesh and blood, He was tempted to sin just as we are. He was One Person worth the entire human race.

Ever since the night of that dramatic escape from the Egyptians, the Passover has been celebrated every year by the Israelites. It became the cornerstone of their faith, a solemn commemoration of God's covenant faithfulness, and a statement of their belief that one day the Great Deliverer Himself would come and crush the oppressor called the serpent. Gradually lambs were bred specifically for the Passover, and at the feast itself, three bags of unleavened bread would be placed on the table to represent Abraham, Isaac, and Jacob. The host would then take out the middle wafer, signifying Isaac, the son of promise, and break it before passing it around to everyone present to eat. Wine was added to the meal but one cup was never drunk. This was the cup for the Messiah, and symbolized their faith that in the fullness of time God would send the Anointed One.

And one year, on the tenth of the month, the very day the Passover lambs were brought into Jerusalem to be examined by the Levites in the courtyard of the temple, Christ entered Jerusalem and was soon being questioned by the Sadducees and Pharisees in the same courtyard. Then came the Passover meal, and the Lamb of God Himself officiated at the last Passover of the Old Covenant which became through His words, in His hands, the covenant meal of a wonderful new contract of grace. Jesus took out the middle wafer of bread, and with growing wonder the disciples would have seen that here was indeed the Son of promise. When He broke it and said: "This is my body," what could He mean but that in some way His body would be broken on their behalf for their benefit? And then He took the cup; the cup reserved for the Messiah, and for a moment their hearts filled with joy. But it turned to grief as they heard Him say,

> *This is my blood of the new covenant which is poured out for many for the forgiveness of sins. I tell you, I will not drink of this fruit of the vine from now on until that day when I drink it anew with you in my Father's kingdom* (Mark 14:24-25 [paraphrased]).

No one had spoken those words since the time of Jeremiah. There was no mistaking it for these men whose whole culture revolved around the idea of blood covenant. Jesus was going to be not only the covenant representative but also the sacrifice on behalf of mankind in an incredible new covenant which would provide forgiveness of sins once and for all. By the shedding of His blood, which bore both the human and divine elements in His nature, the life of man and God would be joined together in an eternal covenant of love. For Jesus was both the covenant sacrifice and the burnt offering, the lamb sacrificed as atonement for sin, and as the spotless Lamb of God He was to pay forever the debt of sin.

It may be that to talk in these spiritual terms draws a veil over the full horror and nightmare of what Jesus was doing. But if we look at Gethsemane, we begin to realize the extent of the price that was paid on our behalf. It is in Gethsemane that the real sacrifice took place, in Gethsemane that the redeeming blood began to be shed, for that was where Jesus really yielded Himself to God's will. And that caused Him such agony that it almost killed Him. As He faced the despair of alienation from God, blood burst from His forehead and God had to send an angel to sustain Him in case He never made it to Calvary. What could have caused Him such desperate agony? Was Jesus afraid to die? No, it wasn't simply the thought of being crucified that made Him sweat great drops of blood. Jesus knew He was the Passover Lamb, and what He could see before Him was the dreadful fire of God's judgment that He was to suffer on behalf of sinful man. Lambs had to be roasted, after all. "Could there be any other way?" He cried out in torment. But no, such was God's love for mankind that He was prepared to sacrifice His only Son so that the law of sin and death might be fulfilled and then abolished.

So Jesus' cry on the Cross, "It is finished," was a cry of triumph, not despair. He had fulfilled all the terms of the covenant. All that He was and all that He had He offered up to God on the cross, and, in return, God made available to us, who are heirs of this covenant, all the righteousness and peace and health of Christ Himself. As we partake of the Lamb through repentance and faith, we receive a new nature; we become a new person in Christ. When God looks at us He sees not our sin, but the righteousness of Jesus who dwells inside us. And when we participate in the Lord's supper, we celebrate the fact that our sins and iniquities are remembered no more, and we proclaim to devils, angels and man that we are now a covenant people. We have within us the treasure of God, Jesus Christ, and on the basis of His righteousness we are able to receive the riches of His life. Remember Jeremiah 31. It is God who makes the promises. We have nothing to give Him. All we can do is rest and say thank you, keeping His commands by the power of His Spirit of love within us.

# The Origins of Sickness

We have begun to see some of the blessings available to us under the New Covenant. Included among them are not only forgiveness but also physical health. Sickness was never part of God's plan, any more than sin, and neither of them have any place in His eternal Kingdom. Sin and sickness originate from the devil. The Bible describes him as a thief, and his whole aim is to rob us of our inheritance, to steal our health and peace and joy. He has usurped the throne of this world and seeks to spread his kingdom of darkness over the lives of men, filling their hearts with evil so that sin, sickness, war and want are generated and regenerated in a demonic cycle empowered from the pit of hell.

> *But thanks be to God! He gives us the victory through our Lord Jesus Christ* (1 Corinthians 15:57).

> *The reason the Son of God appeared was to destroy the devil's work* (1 John 3:5 [paraphrase]).

And Jesus spent most of His time destroying sickness, infirmity, demonic-inspired problems and death.

According to Paul, death is the last enemy to be destroyed(1 Corinthians 15:26) and it is good just to remember for a moment that death is an enemy, not a friend. Yes, death no longer has a sting because we go to be with the Lord, but God never intended us to die. He made us to live forever, dwelling in free fellowship with God, eating from the tree of life(Genesis 2:9 and 17), but through man's disobedience, death entered the world, the enemy that could cut man off from God eternally. Nevertheless God still declares His will for man:

> *With long life will I satisfy him, and show him my salvation (Psalm91:16).*

And He plainly makes it possible for us to enjoy many more years than we usually expect, giving us a foretaste of the time when death will be conquered forever. As Moses told the people of Israel:

> *These are the commands, decrees and laws the Lord your God directed me to teach you to observe in the land that you are crossing the Jordan to possess, so that you, your children and their children after them may fear the Lord your God as long as you live by keeping all his decrees and commands that I give you, and so that you may enjoy long life.* (Deuteronomy 6:1-2).

Three score and ten years was a curse, not a blessing if you read the context in Psalm 90:10.

So, long life is what we should be expecting. I do believe that death is something we can put off as long as we have knowledge to put it off. By keeping God's commands and living by faith in Him we can go on to be "full of years" until we receive from God the message that it is time to come home. Then it should be a question of yielding up our spirit, just as Jesus did. He wasn't killed. He knew His work was accomplished and He voluntarily went to His Father. I would like to be like Moses!

> *Moses was a hundred and twenty years old when he died, yet his eyes were not weak nor his strength gone* (Deuteronomy 34:7).

I know several beautiful Christians who seek to love and serve God in the spirit with all their heart and soul. They pray, they study God's word daily, and at ninety years old they don't wear glasses, they don't need a stick, they have hair on their heads and they are planning to go on like that until they fall asleep in their beds, yielding up their breath to go home to their Lord. That's what I'm aiming for anyway, but if I die prematurely next year, don't think I was deceived, because God's Word convinces me that this is what He desires for His people. Having said that, God doesn't generally get His will more than twenty-five percent of the time! If we look at the parable of the Sower we see that only one of the four types of soil allows God's Word to bring forth fruit. So let's look at a few of the blockages:

> *Hear the Word of the Lord, you Israelites, because the Lord has a charge to bring against you who live in the land:*
>
> *"There is no faithfulness, no love, no acknowledgement of God in the land. There is only cursing, lying and murder, stealing and adultery; they break all bounds and bloodshed follows bloodshed. Because of this the land mourns, and all who live in it waste away; the beasts of the, field and the birds of the air and the fish of the sea are dying.*
> *…my people are destroyed from lack of knowledge"* (Hosea 4:1-3; 6).

What a picture of disunity and despair. Social order has given way to anarchy and war. Bonds of kinship and friendship have disintegrated and people are literally wasting away with sickness, and even the natural world is gripped by suffering and decay. What is the cause? "There is no faithfulness, no love, no acknowledgement of God in the land... my people are destroyed from lack of knowledge." What sort of knowledge is meant here? Surely not intellectual wisdom, which is a rational understanding of facts or ideas; it was a spiritual knowledge which the Israelites were lacking, an acknowledgement of God of His laws and of His provisions. A lack of knowledge of these things could stem from one of two causes:

1. Sin

2. Ignorance and misunderstanding

With the Israelites it was plainly the former.

In the past God had made clear to them how they could enjoy peace, health and prosperity – the choice was theirs – life or death – and they had chosen death.

> *See, I set before you today life and prosperity, death and destruction. For I command you today to love the Lord your God, to walk in his ways and to keep his commandments, decrees and laws; then you will live and increase, and the Lord your God will bless you in the land you are entering to possess.*
>
> *But if your heart turns away and you are not obedient, and if you are drawn away to bow down to other gods and worship them, I declare to you this day that you will certainly be destroyed. You will not live long in this land you are crossing the Jordan to enter and possess.*
>
> *This day I call heaven and earth as witnesses against you that I have set before you life and death, blessings and curses. Now choose life, so that you and your children may live and that you may love the Lord your God, listen to his voice, and hold fast to him. For the Lord is your life, and he will give you many years in the land he swore to give to your fathers, Abraham, Isaac and Jacob*
> (Deuteronomy 30:19-20).

Now the people of Israel obviously knew about God. With religious laws woven into the very fabric of their daily lives, almost every act, on one level, was an acknowledgement of God. But did they know God personally? Did they worship Him in their hearts? Plainly the Israelites in the time of Hosea had rejected all God's moral and spiritual commandments, and had given themselves up to selfishness and greed. By turning away from God, they had cut themselves off from the source of all hope and blessing, thereby choosing death instead of life. Without life and light, they quickly degenerated into darkness and despair.

The plight of the Israelites was an extreme one, brought about by wanton disobedience and pride. Their lack of knowledge of God and His laws was a matter of choice, a deliberate disregard of their conscience. In these circumstances, sin brings with it death. There is a sense in which mercy is shown in fact, for God doesn't utterly destroy them but seeks, through the decay, which they have brought upon themselves, to turn their hearts back to Him. God was not the creator of their suffering; but through disobedience they surrendered themselves to the forces of evil. He utilized it to bring about their repentance. There are several instances in the Old Testament of sin reaping sickness in this way. David evidently knew this connection between sin and sickness. He is explicit as to the source of his own pain and illness which he records in Psalm 38:3-8:

> *Because of your wrath there is no health in my body; my bones have no soundness because of my sin. My guilt has overwhelmed me like a burden too heavy to bear. My wounds fester and are loathsome because of my sinful folly. I am bowed down and brought very low; all day long I go about mourning. My back is filled with searing pain; There is no health in my body. I am feeble and utterly crushed; I groan in anguish of heart.*

Again in Psalm 41:4 he cries:

> *…Oh Lord have mercy upon me; heal me, for I have sinned against you.*

We also read in Numbers 12:

> *Miriam and Aaron began to speak against Moses because of his Cushite wife, for he had married a Cushite. "Has the Lord spoken only through you Moses?" they asked. "Hasn't he also spoken through us?" And the Lord heard this.*

Straightaway God summoned the three of them out to the Tent of Meeting where He appeared in a pillar of cloud. He charged Aaron and Miriam with speaking against His anointed servant, Moses, and His anger "burned against them." When the cloud of His presence lifted, Miriam had been stricken with leprosy. No disease was so associated with shame and dishonour, not to mention fear, for it meant not only pain, disfigurement and ultimately death, but social ostracism as well. This sounds harsh, but the severity of her affliction only matched the seriousness of her offence, for she had criticized the Lord's own servant, thereby rebelling against God's order and authority. Not only that, but pride and greed had made Aaron and Miriam jealous of Moses' leadership and they were seeking to assert themselves as vessels for God's Word.

In total contrast to this self-regard, we read, "Moses was a very humble man, more humble than anyone else on the face of the earth" (Numbers 12:3). And it showed amazing humility and grace to cry out to the Lord to heal someone who had criticized and slandered him. No wonder that the Lord had mercy and restored Miriam after Moses' prayer though her sin alienated her from her friends and family for a while (she was confined outside the camp for seven days, in accordance with the laws for cleansing), and the scene had its repercussions on the whole community, for the people were not able to move on until she had been brought back. This suggests a further aspect of sin-related sickness: it can cause both individuals and those connected with them – family, friends, church, community – to be blocked in their walk with the Lord.

In fact, God had already stated that sin could have such far-reaching effects. In His Ten Commandments, He had declared that they shouldn't bow down to any other gods, for …

> *I the Lord your God am a jealous God punishing the children for the sin of the fathers to the third and fourth generation of those who hate me, but showing love to a thousand generations of those who love me and keep my commandments (Deuteronomy 5:9-10).*

Not only could sin have an effect on the immediate community then, but also the repercussions could be felt years later in subsequent generations. We read in Lamentations 5:7:

> *Our fathers sinned and are no more, and we bear their punishment.*

Like ripples from a stone cast into a pool, so the effects of sin travel ever outwards. This seems to be true even when the sin is unintentional. It illustrates how breaking certain divine laws bring its own consequences. This, God allows to get the sinner's attention so that His perfect order might be re-established. Look at the story of Abimelech. Poor Abimelech. There was nothing wrong with him. He couldn't believe his eyes when Abraham arrived on the scene with a really attractive woman called Sarah, who he said was his sister. He had no idea that Abraham had told his wife to play up to this half-lie because he was terrified of getting killed by someone who wanted to have relations with his wife. Yet despite his ignorance and, in fact, perfectly honourable behavior, he and all his family and household became unable to conceive a child. Fortunately Abimelech was a God-fearing man and he remembered to ask God what the trouble was. When he realized the sit- uation he made restitution by returning Sarah to Abraham and giving handsome gifts to them:

*Then Abraham prayed to God, and God healed Abimelech, his wife and his slave girls so they could have children again* (Genesis 20:17).

It is important to remember that it is not that God is vindictive or is angrily punishing wrongdoing as a judge might sentence an offender. As we have already been seeing, sin puts the individual outside the protection of God, exposing him to the threat of "the fowler's snare and…the deadly pestilence…that stalks in the darkness and the plague that destroys at midday." We find here the beginning of an awareness of the forces of darkness always threatening the covenant world. As yet not fully personalized, Satan's destructive influences were recognized as being ever present to afflict those who stepped outside God's will and protection.

This may seem a very simplistic, even harsh picture, but the situation described in these examples is borne out by medical and psychological fact. The Israelites did not have the scientific knowledge to understand the very real connection between sin and sickness. Doctors and psychiatrists have established the relation between emotions such as guilt, anger, and grief and certain forms of illness; the whole subject of psychosomatic illness centres on the interplay between the emotional and physical realms. Stress is well known to be a contributory factor in medical problems such as high blood pressure and heart disease. Abuse of the body from over-eating, smoking, lack of exercise, and over-work, for example, can directly produce physical disorders. With babies being born with VD, addicted to heroin, and now with AIDS, there has never been more certainty that immoral lifestyles, particularly those that are sexually immoral, may well result in serious illness. And within the Church, there is a growing awareness of the possible physical effects of involvement in the undisputed works of darkness, such as witchcraft, spiritism, and other forms of occult activity. We are reaping what we have sown:

> *…Your wound is incurable, your injury beyond healing. There is no-one to plead your cause, no remedy for your sore, no healing for you…because your guilt is so great and your sins so many* (Jeremiah 30:12-14).

Fortunately, there is hope in the mercy of the Lord if not in anything else.

> *"But I will restore you to health and heal your wounds," declares the Lord…* *(v. 17).*

And God says:

> "...Repent! Turn away from all your offences; then sin will not be your downfall. Rid yourselves of all the offences you have committed, and get a new heart and a new spirit. Why will you die, O house of Israel? For I take no pleasure in the death of anyone," declares the Sovereign Lord. Repent and live!
> (Ezekiel 18:30-32).

What is more, for those of us under the New Covenant:

> In those days people will no longer say "The fathers have eaten sour grapes and the children's teeth are set on edge." Instead everyone will die for his own sin"
> (Jeremiah 31:29-30).

I remember being asked to pray for a child who had a deformity in his feet whilst I was ministering in Ontario, Canada. I knew God said "Suffer the little children to come unto Me," and so I was not expecting any problems regarding the child's healing. However, when I prayed at first for the child to be healed, nothing manifestly happened and as a result I asked the Lord about it. Suddenly a thought came to me: "Ask the parents if they have ever entered a temple or mosque." The parents remembered a time abroad when they had gone sightseeing and had removed their shoes in order to view the temple or mosque. I pointed out to them that this might be construed as an act of worship to "other gods." They immediately repented, and I prayed again for the child, this time his little toes started to grow out and became normal.

True repentance brings healing. But ignorance of this promise of restoration and a misunderstanding of God's Word can prevent us from coming back into a relationship with God and enjoying His blessings once more. We can repent and yet not realize we are forgiven and restored to God's full favour. This is a subtler problem that can afflict us even when we are really trying to do God's will, and it takes two forms.

The first is that we do not read His Word enough, so we are simply unaware of the marvellous provision God makes for our restoration and welfare. There is a wonderful scene in the book The Last Battle by C.S. Lewis in which a group of dwarfs have been so blinded by the monkey god they have been serving, that when released from their stable prison and set before a sumptuous banquet of food they think they are still locked up in the darkness, eating straw and dung. Similarly, even when we have not been consciously disobedient to God, we are conditioned to look at our circumstances through the eyes of the world and to expect only what is humanly and rationally possible. We are like birds still sitting in our cage when the door is left open, so accustomed to imprisonment that we no longer recognize freedom. The devil is hardly going to be the one to point out that we are no longer locked in. Still we live as slaves, still under the bondage of sin and the devil, instead of reigning victoriously as legal heirs to all Christ possessed.

Second, it may be that we have heard these truths with our ears but have not opened our hearts (and spirits) to receive them. We give mental assent to the words that we read in the Bible, but somehow don't really grasp the possibilities of making those promises a reality in our own lives. We have a theoretical faith, not an experiential one. The words of God have not become spirit and life to us, transforming our minds so that we see how we really can live in a realm that goes beyond the limitations of our human understanding.

According to the world's standards and expectations, living in the world means living under a curse – a double curse – sentenced to toil and pain and mortality, cut off from God as Adam and Eve were when they were cast out of the Garden of Eden, and also doomed to failure in keeping every part of God's law:

> ...*Cursed is everyone who does not continue to do everything written in the Book of the Law* (Galatians 3:10).

And the effect of breaking God's law was far-reaching and catastrophic:

> *The Lord will send on you curses, confusion and rebuke in everything you put your hand to...* (Deuteronomy 28:20).

It is possible to be born again and be filled with the Holy Spirit, yet still not experience joy and victory over trials and temptations. This will certainly be the case if we are ignorant of what God's Word says and means:

> *Christ redeemed us from the curse of the law by becoming a curse for us...* (Galatians 3:13)

Many Christians interpret this verse only in its primary sense of forgiveness of sin through the substitute death of Christ on the cross. But in the light of the comprehensiveness of what we have seen given in the New Covenant, new possibilities for victory and fulfilment open up at every turn. For

Calvary releases to us all the promises given to Abraham:

> *He redeemed us in order that the blessing given to Abraham might come to the Gentiles through Christ Jesus, so that by faith we might receive the promise of the Spirit* (Galatians 3:14).

And what does the Spirit do? He puts within us the spirit of sonship that enables us to cry "Abba, Father." Redemption involves so much more than merely being saved from something. **It is what we are saved into which is the exciting thing.** The blessing given to Abraham was to be drawn into a covenant with Almighty God; it was a promise of health, prosperity, peace, and protection – and a Savior who would extend His covenant to the whole world. Not only do we inherit all these blessings, but the curses are now reversed and become promises for us. So now when we read the curses in Deuteronomy 28, we can start to praise the Lord that we are not subject to them any more. I heard a story about a man sentenced to jail for theft. As he was taken into the prison he saw some words inscribed over the gates:

THOU SHALT NOT STEAL.

He hung his head and felt those very words justly condemning him for his offence. During his time in prison he had a wonderful experience of God and repented of all his wrongdoing. When he eventually left prison, he looked back over his shoulder and saw those same words. But this time, instead of a condemnation, he read them as a promise:

THOU SHALT NOT STEAL.

The very curse he had received for breaking the law had now become a blessing that he would never steal again. He was now a new creation with a new heart, and he would no longer give in to the old desires and temptations.

This puts a whole new perspective on life. Instead of being dominated by fear and anxiety, we can now live in security and peace, trusting in the faithfulness of our Covenant God to keep and bless us:

> *You will be blessed in the city.*

I know so many people in the city who live in terror of a bomb exploding in front of them, of being robbed, or ruining their health through pollution or stress. But God can turn these circumstances into a place of joy and rest.

*You will be blessed in the country.*

Rural life doesn't have to mean isolation, power cuts, and snowdrifts.

*The fruit of your womb will be blessed, and the crops of your land and the young of your livestock – the calves of your herds and the lambs of your flocks.*

Are children a blessing? Sadly, I know many families where parents would call them a curse. But if we know that Christ has redeemed us from the curse, then we don't have to wait for our little baby angels to become "terrible twos" and our teenagers to take to drink, drugs, and sex. We can expect our homes to be places of joy and love, and our work and business to flourish.

*Your basket and your kneading trough will be blessed.*

When we first started to live by faith my wife would give away our last packet of tea and trust that God would replenish it. He usually did – with two packets! By giving, we really proved that He was our provider. I remember her telling me one day how she went strawberry picking with the words "Your basket will be blessed" running through her mind. As she went down the rows, she came across a huge basket of strawberries upturned and left, its precious load spilling on the ground. A shame for the other person, but God's wonderful provision for Rosemary! Gone are the days dreading the next invoice, wondering where we will find the money to buy the food and to clothe the children, or constant financial anxiety and strain. Instead:

*The Lord will grant you abundant prosperity*

Suddenly we realize we are plugged into God's limitless resources. He will supply all our needs according to His glorious riches in Christ Jesus, and that's different from having a fat wallet in our hand – it's having a hand in God's fat wallet!

*You will be blessed when you come in and blessed when you go out.*

If we are living under the curse, when we go to work, we expect to be dominated, crushed, humiliated, unfairly treated; at meetings we're looking for problems and spiritual attack; in business, we live in fear of failure; when we travel we are terrified of an accident; when we get home we wonder if we have been burglarized. Redeemed from the curse, we can feel completely secure, for ..*The Lord will keep you from harm – he will watch over your life; the Lord will watch over your coming and going both now and forevermore (Psalm 121:7-8).*

In Deuteronomy 28:22, we read that another effect of the curse of breaking God's law is being afflicted with wasting disease, fever, and inflammation. How many people suffer from stress-related diseases these days? But under God's blessing,

> *The Lord will keep you free from every disease. He will not inflict on you the horrible diseases you knew in Egypt, but he will inflict them on all who hate you* . (Deuteronomy 7:15).

Disobedience and sin can mean that "the heavens above your head shall be like brass" (v. 23). Have you ever experienced your prayers just bouncing back off the ceiling? I've got a way around that now; I say "Devil, it's no good, you lying to me and saying I can't get through and there's a block between me and God, because that's only true under the curse, and, frankly, I'm under the blessing."

When Jesus went from earth to heaven. He carved a great hole right through the principalities and powers of darkness so that there is always a way through to God for me. After praying that truth for about five minutes, I can start to feel the presence of God once more, because the devil just can't deceive me any longer.

> *Then you will know the truth and the truth will set you free* (John 8:32).

When we see that Christ, "having disarmed the powers and authorities, made a public spectacle of them, triumphing over them by the Cross" (Colossians 2:15) we realize that our true position is to be seated with Christ in heavenly places and our whole attitude changes. We can get up in the morning, look in the mirror and say:

> "**You** are more than a conqueror."

For he has called us out of darkness into His wonderful light. We are part of the kingdom of His dear Son. So we don't have to get the flu just because everybody else has it. It's marvellous. A new way of living opens up.

We find another reason why people get sick in Paul's first letter to the Corinthians:

> *The Lord Jesus Christ on the night he was betrayed took bread and when he had given thanks he broke it and said, "This is my body which is for you, do this in remembrance of me." In the same way after supper he took the cup saying,*

*"This cup is the New Covenant in my blood; do this whenever you drink it in remembrance of me. For whenever you eat this bread and drink this cup, you proclaim the Lord's death until he comes."*

*Therefore whoever eats the bread or drinks the cup of the Lord in an unworthy manner will be guilty of sinning against the body and blood of the Lord. A man ought to examine himself before he eats of the bread and drinks of the cup. For anyone who eats and drinks without recognizing the body of the Lord eats and drinks judgment on himself. That is why many among you are weak and sick, and a number of you have fallen asleep. But if we judged ourselves, we would not come under judgment. When we are judged by the Lord, we are being disciplined so that we will not be condemned with the world* (1 Corinthians 2:23-32).

How do we recognize the body of the Lord? The context here reveals at least two meanings. The first involves our understanding of the New Covenant which we have already discussed. God's life flowed out to mankind in Gethsemane and on the Cross. All that God was and has was given to us through the blood of Jesus, winning for us forever the right to physical health as well as free fellowship with the Father through the forgiveness of sins. If we eat the bread and drink the cup of the Lord's supper with this understanding, we proclaim the Lord's death; in other words we make a declaration of faith to ourselves, to the world, to the angels, to the powers of darkness, and to the Lord God Himself, that Jesus' death makes available to us all the fullness and glory of His resurrection life. We need to be aware that when Jesus said, "Do this in remembrance of me," He was using that covenant word, and urging us to hold always in the forefront of our minds the terms of the covenant which entitles us to every blessing of His kingdom. This is why communion should be much more than a memorial service; it should be a means of reaffirming and receiving afresh the fullness of life given to us through the New Covenant.

If we fail to discern the Lord's body in this way, it does not mean that we get sick and weak as a curse or punishment. Rather, we need to realize that there is a law of suffering and death at work in the world generated by the devil, and fuelled by our own sin or ignorance, to which we will be subject unless we positively draw on the life which is the blood. Unless we have a revelation of our entitlement as heirs of Christ in the New Covenant, we will find ourselves subject through deception to the curses which will fall on the world.

We discover the second meaning of discerning the Lord's body in Paul's earlier words about disunity and insensitivity among the believers:

*In the following directives I have no praise for you, for your meetings do more harm than good. In the first place, I hear that when you come together as a church, there are divisions among you and to some extent I believe it…When you come together, it is not the Lord's Supper you eat, for as you eat, each one goes ahead without waiting for anybody else. One remains hungry, another gets drunk. Don't you have homes to eat and drink in? Or do you despise the church of God and humiliate those who have nothing?…*
(1 Corinthians 11:17-22).

*But now in Christ Jesus you who once were far away have been brought near through the blood of Christ. For he himself is our peace, who has made the two one and has destroyed the barrier, the dividing wall of hostility, by abolishing in his flesh the law with its commandments and regulations. His purpose was to create in himself one new man out of two, thus making peace, and in this one body to reconcile both of them to God through the cross, by which he put to death their hostility (Ephesians 2:13-16).*

So there is an even more serious dimension to the sin of not discerning the Lord's body. Unless we recognize that the death and resurrection of the Lord Jesus abolished the barriers of race and custom, unless we love one another, we will be liable to physical sickness and infirmity for refusing to accept the wholeness and order that the Cross won for the Body of Christ. It will be possible then for our physical health to reflect the degree of unity and faith within the Church, both local and universal.

Insensitivity and a lack of love and concern, form a further aspect of taking the Lord's Supper in an unworthy manner and so turning the cup of blessing into a cup of judgment. If I am not in right relationship with my brothers and sisters when I take communion, not only will I not get healed, but I might end up sick if I was healthy in the first place. Some years ago, I took a series of teaching and healing meetings in a traditional denominational church. It was a mini revival. On the first evening, many people were baptized in the Spirit. On the second evening, the gifts of the Spirit broke out spontaneously; and on the third evening, people were healed of arthritis, back conditions and one person even got out of her wheelchair and walked.

Unfortunately, this didn't go down too well with the clergyman's wife who was staunchly traditional and was horrified to see the safe, sedate boat being rocked. I think she could see their sound reputation, along with the minister's pension, just flying out of the window, and she rallied members of like mind within the congregation to resist the "charismatic" influence. It split the church. Now I don't believe it was the people who were filled with the Spirit who caused the rift; it was the traditionalists who created the split by getting terribly upset, insisting that the experiences being claimed were unbiblical, and that someone had to stand for truth in all this deception.

A short time later on another visit, a lady came up to me, glared furiously, and said, "You have totally ruined this church." What a welcome. I was so taken aback I just blinked and said, "I am very sorry." "The only service I enjoy now," she rushed on as if she hadn't heard, "is communion. The only problem is, I can't stand the minister's preaching and I am sure he is not a man of God at all."

On and on she went, criticizing everything about this man and his church. When she stopped to draw breath for a moment, I said carefully, "May I give you a word of warning?"

Needless to say, that was not received. No, she didn't need to be warned, but I stopped her, and explained that I believed I did need to warn her because if she was taking communion and was completely out of fellowship with just about everybody else in the church, she was liable to bring sickness to her body. You can imagine that she was hardly blessed by that and she stormed off. Very soon afterwards she developed rheumatoid arthritis – but sadly she still wouldn't accept that the root of her illness might lie in her criticism and resentment.

Some people will quote John 9 as a reason why they are sick. Here Jesus and his disciples came upon a man who was born blind and his disciples are keen to know whose sin has caused the affliction, the man's or his parents'. But Jesus replies,

> *Neither this man nor his parents have sinned…but this happened so that the work of God might be displayed in his life* (John 9:3).

This verse has sometimes been used to argue that the reason for some suffering is to glorify God, but from what Jesus goes on to say, it seems that He meant that the glory of God is revealed in the man's healing, not his affliction:

> *As long as it is day, we must do the work of him who sent me. Night is coming when no one can work. While I am in the world, I am the light of the world* (v. 4).

Having said this, He went to heal the man, manifesting the power and love of God, and proving in a most dramatic and graphic way that He was indeed the light of the world. So we shouldn't just accept our sicknesses because we feel it is the work of God being manifested through us. No direct work of God could be anything but the vehicle of blessing, joy, peace, wholeness and beauty. God might well glorify Himself through suffering because He can turn every situation into good, but that is only an intermediate purpose. We should be looking for the restorative, perfecting touch of His hand, for that is undoubtedly the work He wants to be revealed in our life.

In our zeal to discover the spiritual roots of sickness, we can easily overlook quite simple, practical reasons why we get sick. If we abuse our bodies in any sort of way, we can hardly expect to remain healthy – unless we have been called to a situation where long, hard hours, lack of food, physical hardship and so on are unavoidable, as in a missionary situation for example. In that case, we can expect God to sustain us miraculously. But we cannot choose to work overtime continuously, go without adequate sleep, take no fresh air or exercise, eat a poor unbalanced diet, have no time for relaxation and still expect to stay in good shape.

It's possible to get sick through our very spirituality, or should I say super-spirituality. We can sometimes get so caught up with the disciplines of prayer and fasting that we don't realize it has become a law to us rather than a work of the Spirit. Either we feel that going without food and praying all night have in themselves some sort of power which acts as a lever to make God do what we want (though we would never admit this, or perhaps even realize that this is a sort of blackmail); or we fast and pray out of anxiety, fearing that unless we mortify our flesh, God won't answer us. No wonder we get sick – and we are almost glad – it's proof for us that our prayers must be doing some good.

We must be on the lookout for another weak area if we are feeling very spiritual. The devil is at his most subtle just when we are rejoicing in the blessings. That's when he slips in, when our guard is down and we have been feeling rather pleased with ourselves. When we have had a few answers to prayers, seen someone healed, led a meeting which has gone well, it is easy to take the credit ourselves almost without realizing it, and to move away from a dependence on God. As soon as we take the glory ourselves and imagine that by our own wisdom and ability we can achieve spiritual success, we are stepping outside God's protection, and particularly in entering "battle areas" like deliverance, we put ourselves at great physical risk.

To summarize, Satan is the originator of all sickness. This world is dominated by his rule of sin, suffering and death, and although we have been delivered out of the kingdom of darkness into the kingdom of our God we live bodily in this world and are threatened constantly by these destructive influences. The enemy is certainly like a prowling lion seeking whom he may devour and unless we consciously appropriate the life God has provided for us and resist what Satan tries to throw at us, we will be subject to all the same physical problems the world groans under. Evidently there is a battle going on, usually in our mind and our emotions.

# The Battleground: Six States of Mind

*What shall we say then? Shall we go on sinning so that grace may increase? By no means! We died to sin; how can we live in it any longer? Or don't you know that all of us who were baptized into Christ Jesus were baptized into his death? We were therefore buried with him through baptism into death in order that, just as Christ was raised from the dead through the glory of the Father, we too may live a new life* (Romans 6:1-4).

*Therefore, if anyone is in Christ, he is a new creation; the old has gone, the new has come!* (2 Corinthians 5:17).

There's something wrong somewhere. Is the world aware that there is a completely different species of human being called Christian on the earth? Or are most of us acting out the fairy tale Emperor's New Clothes, feeling so proud of our wonderful spirituality while the world just laughs at us for being so blind? Clearly, despite all the blessings, all the fellowship, all the teaching, there is still a discrepancy between this radically new life the Bible talks of and the mediocrity of our actual experience.

To a large extent, the problem lies with our minds. Unfortunately, many of us have entered the kingdom of God on the wrong ticket. We accepted Jesus as our Saviour and thought we'd made it. But in fact, nowhere does the Bible speak of accepting Jesus as Saviour **alone**. We need to accept Him as Lord too, and that means a total and continual submission of every aspect of OUR lives. It means coming under a new rule, a new set of laws, a new discipline. It involves willpower – the conscious and constant dedication of our will combined with the power of the Holy Spirit – to bring about our transformation into a glorious new creation.

Some of us have given our heads to God, but we have the same thoughts, the same problems, and the same attitudes as before. We are new Christians, but not fully new creations. When we succumb to the old temptations and difficulties, we start rebuking Satan, asking for ministry, claiming the victory and pleading the blood – but we forget a very powerful little word that God has given us, and that word is No! The Bible is explicit that the old way of thinking, our sinful nature, the "old man," is something we have to cast off. A person I know, after being born again, baptized, and filled with the Spirit, found that his life wasn't really much different. He was still dogged by the same problems and attitudes, but now he was going to heaven with them! Then he had a vision of an Egyptian-type mummy with burial bandages trailing on the ground, walking and talking normally with people. This made him realize that although he was a new spiritual **creation**, he was still dragging around with him all the trappings of his old life, the same habits, thought patterns, and feelings, and he needed to cast them off and leave them in the tomb where they belonged.

God calls us to bring our minds, emotions and bodies under His control. By the power of His Holy Spirit, He is able to mould them so that we grow more and more like Jesus. The Lord doesn't want to erase all the human part of our nature and make us into spiritual robots – Jesus was a person of warmth, energy and intelligence – but He does want these areas to reflect the holiness and purity of His life. Dedicating our lives to God in this comprehensive and practical way is what true spir- itual worship really is. In this position, we are able to receive what God wants for us:

> *Therefore, I urge you, brothers, in view of God's mercy, to offer your bodies as living sacrifices, holy and pleasing to God – this is your spiritual act of worship. Do not conform any longer to the pattern of this world, but be transformed by the renewing of your mind. Then you will be able to test and approve what God's will is – his good, pleasing and perfect will* (Romans 12:1-2).

We need to be honest and recognize that however moral and upright our life has been, we still need to renew our minds. We do not have to overtly manifest selfishness, pride, and a lack of love to show how we have failed to emulate God's character or to hinder receiving His blessings, provision, guidance or healing. Interestingly, the Bible talks of various states of mind by which we are basically governed, and if we can identify our areas of weaknesses, we can offer them up more easily to the Lord to be made new by His Holy Spirit.

There are times when we pray for a sick person, we find him or her unable to receive from God because of a blockage. It is like Noah sending the bird out of the ark and it coming back to him; there is no resting place for the anointing. It may be that the believer failed to renew his mind. The Word of God reveals to us seven different states of mind. There appear to be degrees in these attitudes: the lowest is found in those who totally reject God, and the highest, which affects even the spirit-filled Christian; but all of them represent more steps towards the goal of receiving "the mind of Christ." We will examine more fully what that means, but first let's find out where we are by looking at the six states of mind we might possess before we develop a spiritual mind.

## 1. The Deluded Mind

*The coming of the lawless one will be in accordance with the work of Satan displayed in all kinds of counterfeit miracles, signs and wonders, and in every sort of evil that deceives those who are perishing. They perish because they refused to love the truth and so be saved. For this reason God sends them a powerful delusion so that they will believe the lie and so that all will be condemned who have not believed the truth but have delighted in wickedness (2 Thessalonians 2:9-12).*

A deluded mind is one of the most dangerous states of mind to be in, worse because it believes itself to be enlightened, even one of the chosen elite. A classic example is Jim Jones, the man who caused almost nine hundred people to commit mass suicide in Guyana. Now he wasn't an apparently evil man; in fact he professed to be a born-again Christian, a pastor of a church in Indianapolis of over four thousand people. He became so deluded that he believed he was God, and then he was beyond help. He completely dominated and controlled the minds of his followers so that he was able to make them kill themselves. A normal mind doesn't have that sort of power. Jim Jones had a power similar to Hitler, and he was undoubtedly anointed by the devil.

It is a sobering fact that we will see more and more people with this sort of supernatural power, satanically deluding themselves, who through signs, wonders and miraculous healings will completely deceive thousands and lead them into the pit. It is the Dr. Faustus syndrome. It is possible, perhaps, to reach a point where one is not able to repent, even if one is filled with remorse.

## 2. The Depraved Mind

The tragedy of this state of mind is that often it is found in a person who has had some knowledge of God to start with:

*For although they knew God, they neither glorified him as God nor gave thanks to him, but their thinking became futile and their foolish hearts were darkened. Although they claimed to be wise, they became fools and exchanged the glory of the immortal God for images made to look like mortal man and birds and animals and reptiles.*

*Therefore God gave them over in the sinful desires of their hearts to sexual impurity for the degrading of their bodies with one another. They exchanged the truth of God for a lie and worshiped and served created things rather than the*

*Creator...* (Romans 1:21-25).

The paradox between the intellectual and philosophical acumen of ancient Rome and its blatant immorality and sensuality is well established. Pride in their own understanding and achievements made the Romans self-centred and unable to accept the sacrifice involved in true worship of the Creator. So they lied to themselves and said that by celebrating the pleasures of the physical world – food, drink, sex, the arts, sport – they were worshiping God. In fact, they fell from worship, through religious practice, into mere superstition and eventually they became so deceived that they set themselves up as gods (look at the Caesars who reckoned themselves divine), which gave them license to indulge their sensual passions. So their very wisdom was their downfall, turning them into fools and hypocrites, and finally into creatures less than animals in their perversion, forsaking all appearance of spirituality:

> *Because of this, God gave them over to shameful lusts.... Furthermore, since they did not think it worthwhile to retain the knowledge of God, he gave them over to a depraved mind to do what ought not to be done. They have become filled with every kind of wickedness, evil, greed and depravity...* (Romans 1:26; 28-29).

We need to beware of intellectual and religious pride. Scientists, philosophers, and theologians whose studies should cause them to worship God for the wonderful perfection of His creation and laws can, instead, end up serving the objects of their studies or deifying themselves. And all of us are in danger of doing the same. Materialism, worldly ambition, or sensual pleasure from the very air we breathe, and it is so easy to absorb these values, priding ourselves on our ability and achievement, yet, in reality, becoming ever more foolish. It is a frighteningly short step from that position into depravity. And we can never plead ignorance. No matter how far we sink, we still know we are doing wrong, but we do it anyway. We are perfectly aware that we have broken a covenant but we choose to ignore it and its consequence for the sake of our immediate pleasure. We can try and call our sin a sickness to abdicate responsibility, but deep down our conscience is still alive to the fact that we are deliberately disobeying God. For example, homosexuality is not a sickness; the bible says it is a rejection of God's commandments, and it is sin, however much it might seem like a natural, and therefore, legitimate instinct. Many people are being set free from that problem once and for all if they repent first. But the so-called broad-mindedness, which advocates either uninhibited self-expression, or treats it as an emotional or physical sickness, is in fact the least helpful attitude we can take as it leads people from a darkened into a depraved mind.

## 3. The Feeble Mind

*Comfort the feeble-minded* (1 Thessalonians 5:14 [paraphrase]).

Once we bring our negative thoughts and doubts under control, to overcome the final hurdle and receive the Lord's provision, all we will need are courage and perseverance. All we need! Unfortunately, the idea of endurance is not very popular nowadays, when our society is so geared towards comfort and immediate results. Yet the Bible is full of exhortations to persevere and endure, to hold fast and not to give up:

> *Let us hold unswervingly to the hope we profess, for he who promised is faithful.*

> *So do not throw away your confidence; it will be richly rewarded. You need to persevere so that when you have done the will of God, you will receive what he has promised. For in just a very little while, "He who is coming will come and will not delay. But my righteous one will live by faith. And if he shrinks back, I will not be pleased with him." But we are not of those who shrink back and are destroyed, but of those who believe and are saved* (Hebrews 10:23; 35-39).

We may have to endure suffering from many quarters, from the world in the form of mockery or persecution, and from Satan through sickness, difficulties, temptations, and spiritual attack, but God uses it to bring us to a place of greater blessing by making us more mature in our faith.

> *...We rejoice in the hope of the glory of God. Not only so, but we also rejoice in our sufferings, because we know that suffering produces perseverance; perseverance, character; and character, hope. And hope does not disappoint us, because God has poured out his love into our hearts by the Holy Spirit, whom he has given us* (Romans5:2-5).

A feeble-minded person looks at himself, at his own failings and limitations. Often he has been dominated by an overbearing parent as a child and finds it very difficult to come to any decision on his own. He is easily led, and is vulnerable at being dominated by someone else's will. He is full of self-doubt and anxiety. At the first test of faith, he cries "There, I knew it wouldn't work," and throws in the towel. He is usually first in line for ministry when a new speaker comes to the church. He needs regular counselling sessions with an elder, usually covering the same fears and problems. The feeble-minded person needs to be encouraged (not merely comforted and sympathized with) to **"consider him who endured."** If God has promised, our own abilities or worthiness do not come into it. As Paul urges:

*...Let us throw off everything that hinders and the sin that so easily entangles, and let us run with perseverance the race marked out for us. Let us fix our eyes on Jesus, the author and perfecter of our faith, who for the joy set before him endured the cross, scorning its shame, and sat down at the right hand of the throne of God. Consider him who endured such opposition from sinful men, so that you will not grow weary and lose heart.*

*Therefore, strengthen your feeble arms and weak knees. Make level paths for your feet, so that the lame may not be disabled, but rather healed.*
(Hebrews 12:1-3; 12-13).

Rosemary recalls a picture that flashed into her mind as she was cleaning.

I saw myself when I was at junior school on the playing field. We used to have a special sports day once a year. My favourite race was the egg and spoon because I came in second or third quite often, but I used to fall apart when it came to anything else. I felt I'd lost before I began – there were so many good runners, and I was nearly always one of the last. That didn't do much for my inferiority complex, but this particular day was different. The eager parents were sitting around, all eyes on their children, full of encouragement, and all the girls were there with the teachers, enjoying the sunshine and a day off from classes. Two teachers were at the end of the 100-yard-run holding the white tape. We all got lined up. "On your marks, get set, GO," and we were off! I was doing my best, but instead of giving up as usual when I thought that everyone else was doing better, I kept going. I didn't give up on the inside and think, "Well, I may as well be the best loser." The crowds were cheering, "Go on Rosie!" I got to the tape and looked back – for the first time ever I had actually won! My name was being announced as the winner and I could hear a teacher saying in front of everyone, "Rosemary, you have won the race. Well done! You have won the prize!"

Now this may sound silly but it was just as if it was Jesus speaking to me. He made the announcement. He said I had won! I really laughed. He has already seen me at the finishing post and I am going to receive a prize from Him. How tremendous if we could all see ourselves winning the race God has marked out for us. Then when the devil comes along and says "Give up now, it's too hard," or "You can't make it," we would know that he is a liar.

For the joy that was set before Him Jesus endured the cross and the shame.

We have to encourage ourselves in the Lord and spur on one another. There is a final day coming: He has out His overcoming Spirit in us, and on the day when we meet Jesus face to face, we want to hear those wonderful words, "Well done, you made it. You kept going against all difficulties; enter into My joy."

We must always seek to both comfort and encourage the feeble-minded, as this is what the word of God requires. We may feel like they need a rocket under them to get them motivated but God knows that if they are feeble-minded, they will not have the ability to rise up at that point in their lives. They can only receive love, comfort and encouragement.

We must appreciate that they are, in all probability, close to a nervous breakdown and we must draw alongside to support them and not place additional burden upon their shoulders which could be to their detriment.

## 4. The Blinded Mind

> *Rather, we have renounced secret and shameful ways; we do not use deception, nor do we distort the word of God. On the contrary, by setting forth the truth plainly we commend ourselves to every man's conscience in the sight of God. And even if our gospel is veiled, it is veiled to those who are perishing.* **The god of this age has blinded the minds of unbelievers,** *so that they cannot see the light of the gospel of the glory of Christ who is the image of God*
> (2 Corinthians 4:2-4) [emphasis added].

Have you ever told someone about Christ and have been so excited by the wonder and power of the message that you expected them to fall to their knees in repentance any second until you suddenly realize they are staring at you as if you have two heads? They really haven't understood a word you've said. All the glorious perfection of God's plan for mankind is an unknown language to them. The idea of His love, the sacrifice of His own Son, the need for repentance, God's desire to bless and heal, sounded completely crazy, whilst the concepts of the Virgin Birth and the Resurrection were less credible than fairy stories.

The problem is that their minds have been clouded by the devil, and the arguments that might have moved a person with an open, searching mind will sound incomprehensible to the one whose persistent sin has dulled his ears to the voice of God (see 2 Corinthians 13:14). With a person like this, it is pointless trying to use reason until the scales of blindness are removed from his eyes. And just as God commanded the light to shine out of darkness at the creation of the world, and made His light shine in our hearts (2 Corinthians 4:6), so we need to come against the Prince of Darkness, and command the blindness to be removed so that the person is free to choose light or darkness. If the cause of the blindness lies in some sort of involvement with the occult, this will certainly require the prayer of authority, and even a time of prayer and fasting. After that, we need to "set forth the truth plainly," attacking the dullness and hardness which remain by systematically putting forward the miracle of what God has done, line upon line, precept upon precept, until the shrouds of blindness are stripped away. The gospel is "the power of God for the salvation of everyone who believes" (Romans1:16).

I heard of a church situated in a part of the country where occult practices, covens, and witchcraft were rife. It struggled for months to convince the young people of the town the simplest facts about their lost condition. Although many of these young people had severe problems – they were on drugs, were homeless, or in trouble with the police – they still couldn't see that they were in any spiritual need, and the idea of God's love didn't touch their hearts at all. Eventually a word of knowledge came to the church that the barrier was caused by the satanic practices which had spread a blanket of blindness over the minds of most of the people in the town so that they were unable to respond to the Gospel. When this was revealed, the church had a period of prayer and fasting commanding to quicken this enfeeblement, where at the end they witnessed the most dramatic change. Suddenly there was openness among the young people who shared the Gospel. They seemed to recognize their desperate situation and they responded with sincere repentance to the message of Christ; those who had committed their lives to God were able to receive the truths about His laws and life in His kingdom, and to grow steadily into maturity. Clearly we need to rally against this particular work of Satan – dulling our perception – and say, as it was in the beginning, "let there be light."

## 5. The Carnal Mind

This isn't as awful as it sounds! If you have a carnal mind, it doesn't necessarily mean that you are vicious and immoral, it simply means you have a natural mind, that all your points of reference are based on human ability and understanding, and all your motivation is selfish and directed towards material pleasure and profit. That's not so terrible, that's just human, isn't it? But God didn't create us to be "just human"; He created us to live forever and enjoy free fellowship with Him, and since He is Spirit, we need to worship Him in spirit and in truth (John 4:24).

The New International Version states the case a bit more plainly. Here the "carnal mind" is translated as "sinful mind," and from the context, it is clear Paul is saying that it is perfectly possible to be a Christian yet still possess a sinful nature, yet be controlled by it.

> *Those who live according to the sinful nature have their minds set on what that sinful nature desires; but those who live in accordance with the Spirit have their minds set on what the Spirit desires. The mind of sinful man is death, but the mind controlled by the Spirit is life and peace; the sinful mind is hostile to God. It does not submit to God's law, nor can it do so. Those controlled by the sinful nature cannot please God.* (Romans 8:5-8 [emphasis added]).

Perhaps it is more serious than we thought, then. Unless our sinful mind is renewed, we might end up missing the mark altogether. This is a subtle problem and we need to be aware of the forms it can take. "The mind of sinful man is death." That seems a bit extreme. But we are given the reason in the next sentence: "the sinful mind is hostile to God." A carnally-minded person may appear to be thoroughly good and moral; some of the most philanthropic actions and causes have been fielded by humanists, for example, and all sorts of quasi-religious organizations seem to be showing more constructive love and concern than the true Church. But all the benevolence and idealism can't alter the fact that their minds are thinking independently of God. They are drawing on their own strength and understanding and this limits their effectiveness. And although the universal goal might be laudable, on an individual personal level there is often dissension, corruption, and a lack of inner peace, for only a mind controlled by the Spirit finds true life and peace. Our carnal mind brings knowledge, but it does not bring life!

For others with a carnal mind, God's laws maybe in direct and open opposition to their own desires. Such people admit that they prefer immediate physical pleasure or gain to the "vague" promise of spirit benefits. Again, initially their aims might seem quite laudable – work hard, provide for the family, improve your standard of living, enjoy life to the full – but gradually there is less and less time or motivation to think of other people, their hearts become hardened. The first love and passion to serve Christ soon dies away.

As Christians, unless our sinful mind has been renewed, we will have the outward trappings of spirituality: we will pray, read the Bible, go to church, but we will still be governed by the same thoughts and desires as the rest of the world. And sometimes we do not even realize how much we are fooling ourselves because we have so much head knowledge about God that we think we are actually living it. Chorus-tapes are always on in our homes, we book up for the good conferences, and we talk to people about healing and God's provision, but when illness or difficulties strike we react like everyone else. Why pray when you can worry? Go to the doctor straightaway with your lump, rash, or pain and find out all about it. Why ask God to heal you when it will only take a few days or weeks and a course or two of pills to make you better, or at least take away the symptoms? Why ask God to meet your financial needs when it's so much easier to arrange a loan or an overdraft, or just panic? After all, there's no point in troubling God about it; it's too small (or too large), and anyway, He's not really interested in practical problems, just in getting people saved.

We're being reasonable, rational, and sensible. That's the problem. God is none of these, or at least not by human standards. He works by different laws and to follow Him we need to learn this new way of thinking. God made this plain right from the beginning. In Genesis we read:

> Now the Lord God had planted a garden in the east, in Eden; and there he put the man he had formed. And the Lord God made all kinds of trees grow out of the ground – trees that were pleasing to the eye and good for food. In the middle of the garden were the tree of life and the tree of the knowledge of good and evil.

> The Lord God took man and put him in the Garden of Eden to work it and take care of it. And the Lord God commanded the man, "You are free to eat from any tree in the garden; but you must not eat from the tree of the knowledge of good and evil for when you eat of it you will surely die" (Genesis 2:8-9; 15-17).

Next God created woman, and the man and the woman lived in perfect security, perfect happiness, and complete fulfilment, enjoying a wonderful face-to-face relationship with God. Then along came trouble:

> Now the serpent was craftier than any of the wild animals the Lord God had made. He said to the woman, "Did God really say, 'You must not eat from any tree in the garden'?" (Genesis 3:1).

This is really subtle. The serpent didn't ask, "Did God really say you must not eat from the tree of the knowledge of good and evil?" He was playing on the woman's doubts and confusion. What was it God had said exactly? The tree of life and the tree of the knowledge of good and evil were both in the middle of the garden. Were they really only allowed to eat from one of them? And if so, which one? Satan always tries to confuse and deceive us by calling black, white, and here he capitalizes on the woman's obvious hesitation by implying that the tree of knowledge of good and evil is really the one that gives life:

> *"You will surely not die," the serpent said to the woman. "For God knows that when you eat of it your eyes will be opened and you will be like God, knowing good and evil"* (Genesis 3:4-5).

A clever lie. First, there is only one supreme God; no one can be like Him – almighty, omniscient – as the serpent was implying, as He is unique, the Creator who reigns over everything that He has made. Second, by eating of the tree of the knowledge of good and evil, they would not even acquire the power of Satan. Only if they were to eat from the tree of life would they become immortal. In fact, what happened to them was an unmitigated disaster. Their eyes were opened to their nakedness, and then shame. Next they had to find something to clothe themselves with, and in so doing, they lost their dependence and trust that God would provide all their needs. And finally, when they heard God walking in the garden, they were afraid and hid themselves; fear, guilt and deception dominated man's attitude to God from that moment.

When we see just these immediate effects, we begin to realize why the knowledge of good and evil in the power of man is such a deadly thing. The trouble is that it presents us with a constant choice: is this good, or is this evil? And with our limited wisdom and understanding, and our basically selfish nature, we are tossed about by fears and doubts as we try to make the right decision. It's like trying to measure the length of the Empire State Building with a pocket ruler: we don't have the right tools for the job. If we continue to feed off the tree of the knowledge of good and evil as Christians, we will run into a further problem: double-mindedness.

## 6. The Double Mind

> *If any of you lacks wisdom, he should ask God, who gives generously to all without finding fault, and it will be given to him. But when he asks, he must believe and not doubt, because he who doubts is like a wave of the sea, blown and tossed by the wind. That man should not think he will receive anything from the Lord; he is a double-minded man, unstable in all he does* (James 1:5-8).

Double-mindedness is not a state of backsliding; it is a state of growth. Until we start feeding into our minds the Word of God, we don't have this problem because our thoughts are governed by one human perspective. But when we start to claim the promises of God and live our life according to His laws, the trouble really starts. Because we know we have the flu,

82

our head aches, our nose is streaming, we have a hacking cough and it's going to take a few days, and lots of aspirin, to get over it. But our spiritual thought says, "By His stripes I am healed." So what do we do? Do we give in to our human experience and rational understanding, or do we speak out the real truth, which lies in God's Word, and receive His healing? Bills, bills, and more bills keep piling in, but God's Word promises prosperity and provision. Do we worry and strive or do we rebuke the devil as a thief and a liar, and release God's blessing into our experience? Unfortunately, when we have double-mindedness in a bad way we try to do both!

Let us look together at incidents in the life of Peter:

There's no doubting his enthusiasm and desire to serve the Lord. He really wants to grow in faith, even if it entails walking on water:

> "Lord, if it's You," **[still got a bit of doubt]** "tell me to come to You on the water."
>
> "Come," He said.
>
> Then Peter got down out of the boat and walked on the water and came toward Jesus. But when he saw the wind, he was afraid and, beginning to sink, cried out, "Lord, save me!"
>
> Immediately Jesus reached out His hand and caught him. "You of little faith," He said, "why did you doubt?" (Matthew 14:28-31).

You can just imagine the way Peter had got out of the boat. "Stand aside, James, the Lord's called me. Excuse me, John. It is alright for you to lean on the Lord's chest, but I want some action." And he walked on the water. That was fine, as long as he kept his eyes on Jesus. But when he glanced sideways, he saw the waves getting bigger and a storm brewing. Panic gripped him, and with one bite of the tree of knowledge, he was up to his ears in water. If he hadn't been double-minded, he would have taken a big step in faith that day. But he took his eyes off Jesus and looked at his current natural circumstances and he began to sink.

Or again, when Jesus needed to pay His taxes, He told Peter to go fishing:

> "...Go to the lake and throw out your line. Take the first fish you catch; open its mouth and you will find a four-drachma coin. Take it and give it to them for my tax and yours" (Matthew 17:27).

Peter was a fisherman. This must have sounded insane rather than sound financial sense. He must have felt very stupid going out in his boat that morning.

"What are you doing, Peter?"

"Trying to catch a fish with a coin in its mouth to pay the tax."

But Jesus knew that Peter would have had pride in his ability and knowledge as a fisherman, and unless he was prepared to sacrifice that and to do what appeared foolish to his mind, he would not find the Lord's provision – which cost him nothing, after all, except a little pride.

When God told me to go into the ministry of healing and live by faith, I'm afraid that I told Him He was stupid. As an accountant, I can earn more than most people in the fellowship. I can tithe and keep a missionary on the mission field full-time. It's pointless sending me out in faith. You've picked the wrong man. Send brother so and so. He's out of a job.

God's reply, not unpredictably, was "I do not need your money, but I do need you. And I didn't ask you if it was a good idea. I said it was a God-idea. So do it."

This state of mind is characterized by doubt. Trouble is, we believe our doubts instead of doubting them. We wake up on Monday morning feeling awful and we're tempted to think that the joy we felt in the meeting the night before was all an illusion. God seems a million miles away, and all we can see ahead of us is a day of stress and hassle at work. With faith like this for a bad day, we'll certainly get one. But doubts always come from the enemy, so if we reverse these doubts we will get the truth. It is the devil that makes us think we haven't got any joy. But instead of giving into guilt and condemnation, we should respond: "But the joy of the Lord is my strength. Thank you for reminding me. I don't feel it right now, but I know I've got it. In His presence there is fullness of joy. Well, I am in Christ so I don't just have joy; I have abundant joy. And joy comes in the mornings! I'm going to feel that joy coming through any minute." And by this time, doubt will have to leave, as we will have built up so much faith that we will be able to receive a day of real victory and praise. Jesus said "Man does not live by bread alone, but on every word that comes from the mouth of God." (Matthew 4:4) But how do we change our spiritual diet? The clue lies in Ephesians 6, and the power of God's answer is seen more clearly if we look at it in the King James Version:

84

*Wherefore take unto you the whole armour of God, that ye may be able to withstand in the evil day, and having done all, to stand. Stand therefore, having your loins girt about with truth…* (Ephesians 6:13-14 [emphasis added]).

In 1 Peter 1:13 we read:

*Wherefore gird up the loins of your mind, be sober, and hope to the end for the grace that is to be brought unto you at the revelation of Jesus Christ* (KJV).

The analogy, in both cases, is drawn from the uniform of a Roman soldier. The article was a long shirt made up of eight or nine strips that was worn over the loincloth tied around his waist. This was not the most practical garment, especially in times of battle. When a soldier prepares for battle, he would gather up these strips and tuck them into his loincloth. Then he could run and fight and have freedom to move without tripping over his clothes. So God is saying to us here that when we are being attacked by the enemy, we need to gather up our loopy thoughts and tuck them into our belts of truth. In other words, we need to strengthen our mind by subjecting it to the Word of God. What we see and feel and understand is not the truth; only God's Word gives us the correct perspective on our situation. If we subject our natural thoughts to God's truth, we will find life instead of mere knowledge. "The words that I speak are spirit and life." (John 6:63) And peace: "You will keep him in perfect peace whose mind is steadfast because he trusts in you" (Isaiah 26:3).

The other way to become spiritually minded is to be found in 2 Corinthians 10:3-5:

*For though we live in the world, we do not wage war as the world does. The weapons we fight with are not the weapons of the world. On the contrary, they have divine power to demolish strongholds. We demolish arguments and every pretension that sets itself up against the knowledge of God, and we take captive every thought to make it obedient to Christ.*

Paul may have been using an analogy here, which would have been particularly effective with the Corinthian church. At the time Paul was writing, the Middle East was the granary of the world. Ships laden with wheat and maize would sail along the coast of Corinth bound for the storehouses which supplied the Roman Empire. Hidden in the narrow harbours along the coast were pirate ships that frequently seized these precious cargoes. It was known that these pirates came from the villages that clustered at the top of the steep cliffs above the sea, and eventually a task force of soldiers sailed from

Rome to deal with the problem. At night, they manoeuvred close to the cliffs and threw up grappling irons. Some tiny houses perched right on the edge were actually pulled down into the sea, while elsewhere soldiers swarmed up ropes and took the villagers captive before they had time to flee.

So when we get a thought which sets itself up against the knowledge of God which challenges God's Word or what our spirit feels He is saying to us, we need to send up a grappling iron and pull it down, take that lie captive and make our minds obedient to the law of Christ. There are a frightening number of road accidents in America, and when I drive along there and see a car swerve in front, it's easy to think it could be me next. What do I do when I get that thought? If I say, "Satan, I rebuke you," it usually becomes even more insistent! But what God wants me to do is throw a spiritual grappling iron up, get hold of that imagination as the King James Version calls it, and pull it down. "No, devil. I'm kept by the power of God. He will bear me up even if I dash my foot on a stone." I do not fight the thought, I pull it down. Another time, the thought will come, "This meeting will be a disaster," or "They won't receive you," or "There will be no miracles this weekend." What do I do? I pull it down by saying "They will receive me, they will receive me?" Positive confession on its own is not enough. It's the word of faith – the promise of God applied to the situation – which is effective when I mix it with faith.

Fasting is another way to remove doubt. When Jesus said, "This kind can come out only by prayer and fasting," He meant not so much the deaf and dumb spirit as the unbelief in the disciples. Everything is possible for him who believes. By fasting, we starve our doubts and feed our faith. Starve our unbelief long enough and it will die. Allow it to take root, and it will grow like weeds and strangle our faith. As single-minded people we must renew our thinking and be spiritually minded. For this to happen, we need to feed on God's Word and eat of the tree of life.

Another spiritual aid we often neglect is speaking in tongues. We need to be reminded of this wonderful gift and weapon against enemy strongholds. Paul said he spoke in tongues more than anyone and urged us to pray in the Spirit, and with understanding too. The way to deal with spiritual opposition is by spiritual means, which are effective when used in faith. The Holy Spirit prays through our spirit into a situation that needs changing. Often, as we mature as Christians, this gift is neglected or used only occasionally. We need to stir up this gift and use it much more. We often lose our inspiration because we are bored with the same words or language and forget to put any faith behind the words that we speak. Rosemary and I find that we can speak with new phrases or languages deliberately as well as inspirationally. We can form new sounds, use new vowels and as we have said to people, start anywhere from A-Z, but don't keep repeating the same words. It has been exciting to hear God speak through people in a refreshing way as they experience new languages, even singing out a message in tongues with an interpretation. We need to use these gifts and never let them grow stale. They are for the refreshing and encouragement of those in the church, and the testimony of Jesus to the outsider, and as we speak in tongues in our daily lives more and more it helps our minds to be still and hear God's thoughts. We become strengthened in our inward man. Our mind no longer dominates our spirit but becomes subject to it. Instead of analysing everything and taking it through our computer brain, we are more able to believe and receive from God, and His Word becomes easier to read and understand. As we speak in tongues His Spirit illuminates our way. We begin to get direction in our lives and discernment in many situations whether in counselling, ministry, or for our own personal lives. If people have had a mental breakdown or are feeble-minded, it is especially helpful if they are Spirit-filled Christians, and for them to speak in tongues every day. That way they will become stronger in their minds and healing will come more quickly.

When Paul said he spoke in tongues more than most, he needed to do so because of the circumstances in which he found himself, but also because he knew that in his ministry the power to heal and deliver men and women from demons and sickness laid in the Holy Ghost and he needed to be constantly refilled by Him.

> *We have not received the spirit of the world, but the Spirit who is from God, that we may understand what God has freely given us.*
>
> *This is what we speak, not in words taught us by human wisdom but in words taught by the Spirit, expressing spiritual truths in spiritual words. The man without the Spirit does not accept the things that come from the Spirit of God, for they are foolishness to him, and he cannot understand them because they are spiritually discerned. The spiritual man makes judgments about all things, but he himself is not subject to any man's judgment: "For who has known the mind of the Lord that he may instruct him?"* **But we have the mind of Christ** (1 Corinthians 2:12-16 [emphasis added]).

Alone, we can find it difficult to discern the Lord's mind. But when several people seek the Lord together, He can make His will more clear through a variety of spiritual gifts. As individuals, we tend to see things only from our own particular viewpoint and our vision is often narrow. I may only have a part of God's mind, a partial understanding of His purposes; conversely, you may have another part. As we lay down our prejudices and learn to trust one another, we will become much more effective, and our love and appreciation for one another will deepen. Corporately, then, we discover the mind of Christ, even though we may hold different opinions. This is the mind of Christ: life and peace.

# The Renewed Mind: Looking to Jesus

We say of two people who have just fallen in love, they have eyes only for each other. Oblivious to everything else around him or her, their love for one another makes every glance, movement, and word of their beloved totally captivating. Their vision and thoughts are completely filled by the object of their desire, and this inspires them to noble acts and a disregard of themselves, making even the most mundane of tasks enjoyable.

Similarly, the centre of a baby's world is his mother. His eyes will follow her around the room, dismay crosses his face when she goes out for a moment, and delight greets her when she returns. Most of what he learns — both good and bad — comes from her, and in trouble or pain it is always to her that he looks first.

To learn a difficult skill, the apprentice must do more than read the theory in textbooks. He must spend hours, months, even years, watching the master craftsman until he has learned every intricate movement to reproduce a work of equal quality.

What fills our vision, shapes our minds, and dictates our actions? As Christians, what are our eyes fixed upon and what influences our thoughts and lifestyle? There is no doubt where we should be looking:

> *Let us fix our eyes on Jesus, the author and perfecter of our faith, who for the joy set before him endured the cross, scorning its shame and sat down at the right hand of the throne of God* (Hebrews 12:2).

In the context of healing, I find most people are absorbed by their illnesses. They spend most of their time looking at their symptoms, analyzing their sickness, wondering if it's getting worse, and very little time looking away from their problem to Jesus.

Throughout Scripture we see people being presented with a choice: either look at the problem or look to the Lord. If you look to the Lord, you will find He will do something about your problem. It is so simple that most people reject it because they feel healing cannot be that straightforward mainly because they've already been prayed for by a lot of people and they are just as sick as ever. That was my experience for years. Most people with a healing ministry had a go at praying for me, and coping with the feeling of condemnation and anger afterwards when I didn't get healed was very difficult. I began to think that I didn't have enough faith, or maybe God didn't want to heal me. This is when I realized I was doing one fundamental thing wrong, I was looking for my healing. My mind was focused on my problem – my stammer – rather than on God who heals. The Bible says we walk by faith, not by sight, but that doesn't mean I close my eyes and refuse to look anywhere. It means I fix my eyes on the person who starts my faith, sustains my faith and brings it to perfection – the Lord Jesus Christ. Now when I do this, my sickness stops being mine, my problem by which I almost identify myself, and becomes a problem quite detached from me. Until then, I'm so wrapped up in my sickness that God can't reach past it to heal me.

The Greek verb, which is translated "let us fix our eyes on Jesus" carries the sense of looking **away from** one thing, **towards** another. So we need to pull our attention **away from** our problem and **towards** Jesus. Turn away from our pain and look towards Jesus, away from doctors' reports and look towards Jesus. We must deliberately turn our eyes away from everything which causes us fear and dismay, and fix them on the One who **is our healer.**

Remember Moses at the waters of Marah? We saw how he had to look away from the complaints of the people and the impossibility of the situation; he had to keep on looking to the Lord even in the face of what seemed a ridiculous answer to the problem. But by doggedly fixing his eyes on the Almighty God, he seemed to create a channel for the Lord's provision, and brought about the wonderful revelation of the Lord's healing purpose towards His people.

The same principle is illustrated a little further on in the Israelites' wanderings. Surprise, surprise, they were moaning again:

> ... *"Why have you brought us up out of Egypt to die in the desert? There is no bread! There is no water! And we detest this miserable food!" Then the Lord sent venomous snakes among them; they bit the people and many Israelites died. The people came to Moses and said, "We sinned when we spoke against the Lord and against you. Pray that the Lord will take the snakes away from us." So Moses prayed for the people. The Lord said to Moses, "Make a snake and put it on a pole; anyone who is bitten can look at it and live"* (Numbers 21:5-8).

Faith comes by hearing, and when God spoke to Moses he knew that he must trust God to work through this unorthodox way. But can you imagine the reaction of the Israelites when Moses hoisted a bronze serpent up on a pole and promised they would be healed if they looked at it? Time was running out. That's the trouble with snakebites. You can tell exactly how long you've got before you die by how far your body has swollen with the venom. So if you have a leg the size of a tree trunk, there's no time to play games. But since the nearest hospital was forty years away and you had to be a good swimmer to cross the Red Sea, most of the Israelites decided they had nothing to lose. (And I think that is why a lot of people with incurable illnesses get healed while people with colds still struggle; when you are desperate it's much easier to be whole-heartedly committed to God's way.)

Again, neither Moses nor the Israelites knew that the snake on the pole pre-figured Jesus crucified on a Cross, fulfilling His Prophecy:

> *But I, when I am lifted up from the earth, will draw all men to myself* (John 12:32).

They didn't know that by the stripes of Jesus they were healed. They would never see Jesus spread out His arms on the Cross and cry, "It is accomplished." They were simply being obedient, looking to a snake on a pole rather than relying on their own abilities or human under- standing. And not one died!

> *…Then, when anyone was bitten by a snake and looked at the bronze snake, he lived* (Numbers 21:9).

When your mind tells you that you are sick, and it is very difficult to **deny** yourself, to look away from all your feelings, the physical evidence, the negative remarks (You really do look awful…), to look to the Lord.

I have a Catholic friend who had been crippled for thirteen years. She had never been taught to read her Bible and so she did not have much confidence in the idea that God could heal her, but eventually some friends persuaded her to go along to renewal church service. There all the Christians gathered around her and started to say "Sister, you can be healed. You can get out of that wheelchair and walk." Well, she was terrified. She had some bones in her feet that wouldn't stop growing and her feet were incredibly painful and extremely deformed. She knew there was no way she could get up and walk. So she told them she wanted to be alone and talk to God. Pushing her wheelchair down to the front of the sanctuary, she found a huge crucifix on the wall, and her eyes were riveted to the nailed feet of Jesus on the Cross.

"Oh Lord," she cried, "Your feet are just like mine and yet You never once complained. I've spent thirteen years complaining. Please forgive me. Lord.

I'm sorry, I didn't realize how You suffered and that I could have the privilege of suffering like You."

She had never known God in a personal way, but her heart was right, and suddenly she found she just couldn't take her eyes off the feet of Jesus. The next thing she knew, a wonderful heat came over her head, down through her spine, through her legs and bathed her feet in tremendous warmth. As it did so, all the pain left and she cried out, "Oh Lord, you've given me such grace to suffer. I can't even feel the pain"!

That gave God another problem because she was healed and didn't know it! She left the church that night still in her wheelchair, and three weeks later she was still thanking God she was able to suffer her disability without pain. Then one day her three little children got into a fight together and the two little boys came in with bleeding noses. Without thinking, the mother stepped out of her wheelchair to comfort them and they all shrieked, "Mummy! Look at your feet!"

There she stood on two perfectly normal, healthy feet – and since that happened in the early '70s, she has never been back in a wheelchair.

Some years later, at an annual check-up, her doctor told her the devastating news that she had a malignant tumour in her womb.

"I'm very sorry but we'll need to remove the womb as soon as possible. You'll have to come in for surgery tomorrow."

Despite her protests, he was adamant, so she went home to pray about the matter with her husband. Getting on her knees, she cried to the Lord, "What shall I do Lord?"

"Go to the prayer meeting on Thursday night."

That meant postponing her hospital admission, but she went to the meeting where I happened to be preaching about Moses lifting up the bronze snake on the pole in the wilderness. All that had happened some years before came flooding back and she thought, "That was how I got healed last time. If I got healed then without knowing how it worked, now I can co-operate with God and receive again." And she started to look towards Jesus, reaching out to Him in her spirit and really clinging to Him. Now I had no idea she was in the meeting, but just at that point I had the strangest word of knowledge I have ever had: "It feels as though I have a six-pound cancerous tumour in my womb."

92

I wasn't quite aware of what I was saying as this feeling was so real, a great bulge in the pit of my stomach. And then equally suddenly, the word came to me that somebody halfway back in the hall was being healed. Up shot her hand, and instantly the power of God went right through her and she lost six pounds in weight just like that.

Now her doctor was sitting next to her, and he was not amused. He came forward after the service and said, "I like a good preacher, and I wouldn't put you in that category at all. When it comes to healing, why don't you leave it to the experts? After all, how can you heal anybody?"

"I cannot heal anyone "I replied I couldn't heal a fly with a headache, but Jesus can and does still heal people."

Not surprisingly, he wasn't cheered up by that remark, and he urged the woman to come into the hospital for surgery the next day. She prayed about it and felt she should go in to prove to him there was nothing wrong. So she went in and he examined her for fifteen minutes with tears pouring down his face. Saying: "I cannot find it! What's happened? I do not know how he did it. I do not know how he did it."

To which she replied, "He didn't do it, Jesus did."

In the face of such evidence, the poor doctor had to give in and he too, eventually committed his life to Christ.

What is it about looking to Jesus that is so effective? Again I emphasize I'm not talking about just positive thinking or some mystical creative power released through the imagination. What I am encouraging you to discover is the redemption that is yours through the blood of Jesus:

> *For you know that it was not with perishable things such as silver and gold that you were redeemed from the empty way of life handed down to you from your forefathers, but with the precious blood of Christ...* (1 Peter 1:18-19 [emphasis added]).

As I have meditated on this verse, the Lord has pointed out how Jesus' blood was shed from certain parts of His body, and each of His wounds bears a particular significance for us. In Luke 22, we find Jesus praying in Gethsemane:

> *"Father, if you are willing, take this cup from me; yet not my will, but yours be done." An angel from heaven appeared to him and strengthened him. And being in anguish, he prayed more earnestly, and his sweat was like drops of blood falling to the ground* (vv. 42-43).

Jesus knew exactly what physical agony He would endure on the Cross. Crucifixions were a common sight along the roadside, and victims suffered a ghastly slow, torturous death, finally dying of suffocation after days of pushing up from the nails in the feet to try and draw breath. But His turmoil in the Garden of Gethsemane was not so much because of the physical pain that awaited Him, but because He was already experiencing the mental and emotional agony of bearing the punishment for sin for all mankind, the supreme agony of complete separation from God. Terrible even for us to imagine, but for the Son of God, who had always enjoyed perfect fellowship with the Father...for the Light of the World to be plunged into utter darkness for our sake...impossible to imagine the pressure that caused the capillaries across His forehead to burst and great drops of blood to mingle with His sweat. Apparently, there is an actual medical condition, which verifies what happened and, significantly, it is only Luke, the doctor, who includes this detail in his narrative.

With this blood, Jesus was sweating away His very life and became so weak that God had to send an angel to strengthen Him before He died without ever reaching the Cross. What is the significance of the blood Jesus shed in Gethsemane? I believe one of the purposes of this particular agony was to help us find healing for emotional problems, depression, mental illness, mental handicap, migraines, and all types of brain disorder. Not that God compartmentalizes healing in an "eye for an eye and a tooth for a tooth" kind of way – but by concentrating on a specific aspect of Christ's suffering, we quicken our faith.

Since I started preaching this aspect of truth I have seen hundreds of people who suffered from dyslexia and related problems healed by the power of God. Jesus' head was damaged so that any problem in anyone's head can also be healed.

What Jesus has done for us becomes more real and powerful as we use our spiritual perception, to see and understand that His pain was suffered so that we might be healed. Instead of looking vaguely at Jesus, we can zero in on specific aspects of His suffering, which are relevant to our own problem.

> But He was pierced for our transgressions, he was crushed for our iniquities; the punishment that brought us peace was upon him, **and by his wounds we are healed** (Isaiah 53:5 [emphasis added]).

By shedding Jesus' blood, God has already provided for our healing. "It is finished," Jesus cried out on the Cross. Nothing more needs to be done from God's point of view; we simply need to know how to receive that gift.

So, when I have a blinding migraine, I can look at Jesus' drops of blood that were shed in Gethsemane, and also to His head pierced by a crown of thorns, and I can say:

94

"Lord, I have this terrible pain in my head but thank You that You paid the price for me to be free of it for ever. Your head ached more than I could ever imagine. So I'm not going to trust in my remedies I am going to trust in You. I'm not going to fight the devil; I'm not going to rebuke him all the time and give him all the attention. I'm just going to trust You and receive what You won for me."

And you will be healed if you do this. You might "die" a little because it might not be immediate, and you will have to cling on, denying your feelings and doubts, but that is what commitment is all about. Don't just glance at Jesus. **Fix your eyes on Him and do not let Him go.**

I first heard this message from a friend of mine, Roger Price, and it started a whole new thought process in my mind. The first night I preached it, somebody came to the service with a retarded child. He could neither read nor write, he had no creative thought processes, and was aggressive, hyperactive, and allergic to all sorts of food. I didn't feel particularly full of faith, but I just prayed for him, remembering the precious blood spilled from Jesus' forehead and asked God to heal him. There was no visible change there and then, and his parents took him home, but the next morning he started singing choruses, something he had never done before though he had been taken to church every Sunday for years. Not only that, but he came downstairs having dressed himself for the first time in his life. His parents, overjoyed, decided he must be healed and so they allowed him to eat all the food he was allergic to – with no adverse reactions at all. They sent him to school and within weeks he could read and write, his teachers were amazed. Six months later, they took him to the Children's Hospital and he passed every single test the specialist gave him. Today he loves Jesus and wants to be an evangelist.

If we go on from Gethsemane to John 19, we find Pontius Pilate ordering Jesus to be flogged. This was a dreadful punishment. Jesus would have been strapped by His hands to the whipping post, and an instrument like a cat-of-nine-tails, with nine strips of leather ending in pieces of glass would have lashed His back. We don't know how many times they scourged Him, but it would have been at least thirty-nine, as Jewish law said forty save one, and Roman law had no limit. But what we do know is that His flesh was so stripped away that His back looked like a ploughed field, for we read:

*"Ploughmen have ploughed my back and made their furrows long"*
(Psalm 129:3).

Why did Jesus have to endure that terrible pain of having His back torn to shreds? Again, it was so that His wounds might heal us. His blood was shed for our physical healing. If you are suffering from some back problem, try picturing the torn back of Jesus and see His blood flowing out to give you life. In fact, if you are sick in any way, always meditate on these things, or if you are praying for someone who is ill, always minister the Word to them first for: *"Faith comes from hearing the message, and the message is heard through the Word of Christ"* (Romans 10:17).

The suffering of Jesus teaches us to have faith in the laying on of hands, prayers for the sick, and anointing with oil. All are ways God can use to bring healing to those who seek Him in faith. It was Jesus who sweat drops of blood in Gethsemane; Jesus who went to the whipping post and endured His back being lashed raw; Jesus who had His coat stripped from Him and a crown of thorns pressed onto His head; Jesus who was thrown against a piece of wood and had nails driven in His hands and feet; Jesus who hung in excruciating agony on the Cross with a spear wound through His side; Jesus who cried, "My God, my God, why have you forsaken me?" so that we could be healed of our sicknesses, rejection and pain. Jesus. Jesus was our substitute in every way. He was rejected so that we might know acceptance. He was made sin so that we might have His righteousness. He was a man of sorrows so that we could have His joy. He died so that we might have His life. His body was broken so that ours could be made whole.

Receive. It sounds so simple but some of us don't know how to receive. We only feel comfortable if we are giving or doing. We need to look at some of the groundwork we might have to do before we get to the point of being able to receive our healing.

# How to Receive your Healing

Assuming that you have understood the provision God has made for your physical health through His New Covenant, and seeking with His help to renew your mind, there are five steps which may help in preparing you to receive your healing. They are not necessarily chronological or even essential because God doesn't work according to a manmade set of rules, but if followed, they will put you in a position of faith and expectancy.

## 1. Confess Your Sin

> *Therefore confess your sins to each other and pray for each other so that you may be healed. The prayer of a righteous man is powerful and effective* (James 5:16).

The problem with unconfessed sin is not so much that God withholds blessing, as that a tender conscience or a feeling of guilt makes it very difficult for us to expect to receive anything from God. It's not impossible to get healed while still walking in sin because God's grace abounds to us, but it is a lot easier if we obey God's commands, repent of our sins, confess any harboured resentment or bitterness, and walk in the light with God and our fellow men. The result of such action is that our prayer becomes powerful and effective as we become an open channel for the full force of God's love. As a precaution, I would say that we shouldn't become self-analytical and grope around for hidden sins or wrongful attitudes. If we have an honest and open relationship with God, we can keep looking to Him and His light will illuminate any dark areas in our lives.

## 2. Offer God a Sacrifice of Praise

This may seem a strange thing to do, and I do not mean that we should welcome sickness, for we have already established that all illness comes from the devil. But sometimes we are so bound by fear about our condition that our identity is bound to our sickness. It is as if the sickness possesses us, rather than us having the sickness. I'm a diabetic, we say, rather than I have diabetes. I am arthritic, rather than I am a person with arthritis in the hips or legs. By offering to God a sacrifice of praise, we can become more God-conscious and thereby realize that our person and our current condition are not synonymous. Also praise deals with any fear that we might be experiencing.

## 3. Build Yourself up in Faith

One famous preacher described this process as getting pregnant in the spirit. Faith for your healing may start as a tiny seed within you, but as you feed it, this seed will grow and grow until the unseen and hoped for becomes a reality. We can feed our faith in several ways:

**a.** To remove your doubts and your dependence on your own understanding, pray and praise in tongues. There is nothing like it for lifting up your heart and giving you joy and confidence, enlarging your vision of what God can do, and getting rid of your negative thoughts. Look at the effect praise had on Abraham:

> *Against all hope, Abraham in hope believed and so became the father of many nations, just as it had been said of him, "So shall your offspring be." Without weakening in his faith, he faced the fact that his body was as good as dead – since he was about a hundred years old – and that Sarah's womb was already dead. Yet he did not waver through unbelief regarding the promise of God but was strengthened in his faith and gave glory to God, being fully persuaded that God had power to do what he had promised* (Romans 4:18-21).

Praying in tongues and praising God form part of the process of renewing the mind as we have already seen. By doing this, our spirit is allowed to control our mind, rather than our minds controlling us. Supernatural things become natural to us. I always supposed that Christians automatically heard God, but if I were honest I would have to admit that He did not seem to be speaking to me. It took me eighteen months of speaking in tongues, for one and a half hours in the car to work and one and a half hours on the journey home before I heard God's voice. Eighteen months of washing my mind with the Spirit to get rid of all the doubts, fears, and scepticism of twenty-eight years of living by my human limitations. I became a Christian at the age of twenty-three, but it was five years later that I really started to feed from the tree of life myself, though I was ministering healing to others who were more open to God long before I personally experienced healing.

**b. Listening to tapes and reading books on healing** will quicken your faith still further. Even if you have read a particular book ten times before, you will find something new to encourage you on the eleventh reading. Our minds are being bombarded every moment by negative or unhelpful suggestions that it is only sensible to counteract their influence with words of faith.

**c. Meditating on God's Word** will not only increase our faith but may also be the direct channel of God's healing when His Spirit anoints it. As we read in Proverbs 4:20-22:

> *My son, pay attention to what I say; listen closely to my words. Do not let them out of your sight, keep them within your heart;*

> *for they are life to those who find them and health to a man's whole body.*

Meditating on Scripture doesn't mean merely reading our daily quota of verses and absorbing it simply with our minds. Nor does it mean clearing our minds and waiting for something to drop into it. To meditate on the Word means to **chew** on it, to feed on it.

Man does not live on bread alone but on every word that comes from the mouth of God. In fact, the Hebrew carries the sense of regurgitating like a cow chewing the cud – taking the Word down, digesting it, bringing it back up, chewing on it again and taking it down. And eventually the Word becomes part of us, just as food is converted into energy and builds our muscles, renews our body tissues, strengthens our bones.

For example, if I were going to meditate on "by his wounds, you have been healed," (1 Peter 2:24) I would first take the words "by his" and dwell on them for five or ten minutes: "Lord, thank You; all my healing comes from You; only through Your perfect sacrifice can I have life..." Then I would move on to the word "stripes" and picture Jesus strapped against the whipping post being scourged for my healing, Jesus bleeding on the Cross so that I could be free from pain. Next I would think about the word "you." That means me! "Thank you, Lord, You simply didn't do this for everyone else in the world but You did it for me, too. Your love for me is so great; You care for me individually, personally." Then I would spend about ten more minutes meditating on "have been," because this is the difference between being sick and being healed: it has been accomplished! Jesus did everything necessary for my health nearly 2,000 years ago. By the time I get to the word "healed" I am generally strong enough in faith to believe it.

Jeremiah said,

> *When your words came, I ate them;*
> *they were my joy and my heart's delight...* (Jeremiah 15:16).

> *A cheerful heart is good medicine...* (Proverbs 17:22).

As Paul and Silas praised God in prison, with their backs raw from being whipped and their feet in stocks, joy filled their hearts and the power of the Lord fell with a tremendous force that it caused an earthquake. The prison doors flew open, and the jailer threw himself trembling at their feet, begging to know how he could be saved. So not only were Paul and Silas freed from bondage and eased of their physical suffering through their praise, but the father and all his family found salvation.

> *Then they spoke the word of the Lord to him and to all the others in his house. At that hour of the night the jailer took them and washed their wounds; then immediately he and all his family were baptized* (Acts 16:32-33).

So we see how powerful and comprehensive the healing is that lies within the anointed word.

Other helpful verses to meditate upon are:

> *[He] forgives all [my] sins, and heals all [my] diseases* (Psalm 103:3).

> *But for you who revere my name, the sun of righteousness will rise with healing in its wings…* (Malachi 4:2).

> *…He took our infirmities and carried our diseases* (Matthew 8:17).

> *…I will heal my people and will let them enjoy abundant peace and security* (Jeremiah 33:6).

Because of the value of meditation, it is a good idea to **seek the Lord daily for a word from the Bible** for our situation. The children of Israel had to gather fresh manna each day to sustain themselves or else it decayed and produced worms. So we need to feed off fresh words each day and not rely on yesterday's promise because it will become stale and lose its anointing. We don't have to receive a new word every day but to receive it in a **fresh** way.

A long time ago, I had to take a healing service and just before it I developed a prolapsed bowel – not the easiest of afflictions when you have to preach for hours. I was in agony standing up, and in worse pain sitting down, so I was in real trouble. My first thought was to cancel the healing service and get myself into a hospital, but then I considered that Jesus didn't do that so neither could I. Then I decided that God would surely heal me as soon as the service started, so I staggered up to preach and endured three and a half hours of acute pain, hardly able to move. When I crawled home to my wife, I climbed into bed feeling very sorry for myself and said weakly, "Please pray for me, darling."

Her reply was not exactly a blessing at the time.

"There's no point. You know too much. If you were going to preach healing, you'd better live in it. Get a word from the Lord."

Great encouragement! Well, it was obvious I wasn't going to get any sympathy so I had no choice but to seek the Lord myself.

"Lord, I'm desperate," I prayed. "I'm tired. I'm in pain. I'm fed up, and I feel like I'm dying. Please speak to me."

So I opened my Bible and the first verse I read just shot out of the page and hit me: "I will come and heal you."

This was tremendous! A *rhema* word, a God-breathed word that flew like an arrow straight to my spirit and made my faith leap up. All the nagging doubts and fears about whether I should have been sensible and gone to the hospital suddenly faded. That night I went to sleep like a baby.

The next morning I woke up with the thought, "I must be healed." One movement and I realized I wasn't. The pain was still there and stayed with me all day. I couldn't understand why I wasn't on the previous day's word. But like the manna in the wilderness, on the second day it was full of worms. Not just worms, but doubt and unbelief. Did I really get that from God? Was that really what He was saying? When would He come and heal me. It was hopeless. I had to get on my knees that evening and seek God for another word. Another Scripture fired me with faith and expectancy once more. Next morning I still wasn't healed, but now I had gone from doubt to faith, and I just had to go from that place into deeper faith, from glory to glory, until I could receive my healing; I praised the Lord, I spoke in tongues, I sang in the Spirit, and as I was in the presence of God. I said, "Lord, speak to me again. Send me Your word." I could hardly believe my eyes when a verse seemed to leap from my Bible: "Your health will spring forth speedily; I the Lord am your rear reward."

What a word for a prolapsed bowel! I was so filled with joy that I just forgot about my problem, and it wasn't until the next day when I was halfway across the Atlantic in a jumbo jet that I suddenly realized that I had been sitting in one place for four hours and I had no pain. I could not tell you when I had been healed exactly, but at some point the Word had passed from my spirit into my body and brought life and health.

## 4. Enter into the High Praises of God

Doubt and negative thoughts do not come merely from our unrenewed mind; they are often fed to us by the enemy, and one of the best ways to defeat these attacks is to enter into the high praises of God (Psalm 149:6). With the high praises of God are in our mouths, we take up a double-edged sword against the enemy. We enter into spiritual warfare for God inhabits the praises of His people; and when we enthrone Him in our praise and worship, Satan is cut down from the position of power he has usurped. The high praises of God declare to the principalities and powers of darkness that we are not under their dominion, that we belong to Jesus Christ and through our God we will do valiantly.

Now the high praise of God is not a gentle chorus or a sweet melody in the Spirit. It is the people of God joining together and shouting the glory of God into the face of the obstacle. Most of us find this idea very difficult because we want to be seen as normal, decent, and respectable people. Nothing too extrovert or extreme. But if we do not shout the praise of God sometimes, we can be gripped by fear about our sickness. A shout of triumph closes the door on fear and renders the powers of darkness ineffective, for its purpose is to *"bind their kings with fetters, their nobles with shackles of iron"* (Psalm 149:8).

I have seen two wonderful examples of this at work. A pastor telephoned me and asked me to come and pray for a little seven-month-old baby who was in hospital on a life-support machine. He said he felt so condemned because he didn't have faith to pray for the child himself. And I replied that God had been speaking to me about "High Praises" and I suggested that we should call the church together and spend two hours singing the high praise of God to declare to the principalities and powers that Jesus Christ is Lord, and to put the singers out in front of the troops to inspire the army and demoralize the enemy. The whole church gathered at once, and praised into the face of the devil, prophetic praise stripping him of his power in the situation and making a pathway for God to move.

Sometime later I received another telephone call from this pastor who described how he had gone to the hospital the next morning after this spiritual warfare of high praise. He found all the machines had been switched off and the baby lay asleep peacefully. A short time later, she went home, perfectly well. The high praise of God removed all our doubts and broke the devil's hold so that God was able to heal her.

Following that event, I was up in Edinburgh, Scotland where a lovely Christian lady was desperately ill with systemic lupus. She was so close to the Lord that I was a bit concerned she would just slip away to be with Him. However the whole church came together and praised and praised far into the night. That Sunday she stood up in the service and testified to her complete healing and restoration, though no one had actually prayed for her at all. Today she is perfectly fit and healthy, a spoil of war if you like, taken by force from the enemy's stronghold through the high praises of God.

## 5. Rest and Receive

I was travelling in Sweden some years ago, and one day I was invited with another minister to a certain lady's house for coffee and cakes. On the table was a plate of cakes that looked rather like English muffins, not terribly inspiring but all right if there is nothing else!

What caught my eye was a cake sitting right in the centre of all the cakes. It was delicious looking, about four inches wide and an inch high, piled high with lashings of fresh whipped cream and topped with green marzipan. This was appropriately called a "princess cake" and was certainly the most royal-looking confection I have ever seen. I could just imagine that delicious marzipan melting in my mouth, and closing my eyes quickly, I claimed that cake in the name of Jesus. When I opened my eyes, the Swedish pastor had already reached out and taken the cake plus a couple of other cakes and had placed them calmly on his own plate. I was horrified. How ill mannered could he possibly be? But I discovered soon afterwards that Swedish custom was more biblical than British custom. In Britain, we regard it as good manners to take just one cake at a time and always the one nearest to you whether you like it or not. But in Sweden you take the cakes you like best and help yourself to all you want.

When I discovered this, I realized there was a great difference between claiming and receiving. I had bound that cake to the plate in the name of Jesus, but it was the Swedish pastor who had reached out his hand and taken it. Most people are like that at a healing service. When a word-of-knowledge comes that there is a person with an obvious and serious complaint, the individual concerned will turn around to see if anyone else has the same affliction, unwilling to claim the healing in case it belongs to somebody else.

But in Africa, ten people shout immediately, "That's me," and they all get healed! In Britain we are so polite and reserved, but I wonder if that is not really just a cover-up for unbelief. Are we really saying that we do not have enough faith to be healed, so we will pass it on to someone else who has the same problem?

According to Psalm 23, God prepares a table before us in the presence of our enemies. When we are attacked by sickness, God spreads a table with gifts of healing and says, "Help yourself. It isn't waitress service in the Kingdom of God, it is self-service!" We reach out our hand of faith and receive our healing. How do we know we have received it? Well, it is rather like being pregnant. When a woman conceives she doesn't look any different at first, but her thoughts change and her conversation with her husband changes because they are now living with the certainty that they are going to have a family.

When we receive the living Word of God, a seed of faith takes root within us and we have a confidence that we are going to see the fruit. So we must not simply close our eyes and claim our healing, but reach out and take the word down into our very being. When we are claiming, we are often striving, gritting our teeth and almost willing a miracle to happen. When we receive, we enter into rest.

I had a wonderful illustration of this a few years ago. I was speaking in a large church in America. I was talking about the man with the withered arm in Mark 3, and suddenly through the hushed air came the sound of snoring. I've had various comments on my preaching but no one had ever gone to sleep before! At the back of the church, a young woman had nodded off in her seat and was peacefully snoring away. The man next to her was very embarrassed and, giving her a nudge, whispered, "Sister, wake up." Bewildered, she struggled to open her eyes just as I had reached the point in the story where Jesus commands the disabled man, "Stretch out your withered hand" and was explaining that when God tells us to do something we must do it. Half-asleep, half-awake, not trying to understand how it all works – the perfect position in which to get healed – the poor girl thought I was speaking to her, so she stretched out her shrivelled arm which hadn't grown since she was four and a half years old. Suddenly it started to grow and grow until it was completely straight and strong except for one little finger which was still bent over. Tears streaming down her face, she came running out to the front, crying, "Look, look!" I didn't realize what had happened, so I simply replied, "Yes, I've got two like that."

"No, you don't realize that when I came in, it was just useless. When I was about four years old I was playing outside and ran in the way of my father's car as he was turning into the driveway. As a result my arm was badly crushed."

This young woman had a non-Christian husband, and she went straight home, picked up the baby with the arm that had been damaged and waited for him to come back. There was no problem about him receiving Christ.

Having established all these principles, we need to add that everybody will get healed in a slightly different way. And we may find it frustrating that non-Christians seem to get healed comparatively easily, while those more mature in the faith will sometimes continue to struggle. The reason for this may be that God heals the non-Christian to prove that Jesus is Lord, but sometimes heals the more mature Christian when he or she proves to Him that Jesus is Lord. From those to whom much is given, much is also expected and it may be necessary to act out our faith.

In Scripture God implies that the church is divided in a sense into three groups:

> *I write to you, dear children, because your sins have been forgiven on account of his name.*
>
> *I write to you, fathers, because you have known Him who is from the beginning.*
>
> *I write to you, young men, because you have overcome the evil one. I write to you, dear children, because you have known the Father*
>
> *I write to you, fathers, because you have known Him who is from the beginning.*
>
> *…I write to you, young men, because you are strong and the word of God lives in you, and you have overcome the evil one* (1 John2:12-14).

From this it seems that God distinguishes three groups: not Catholic, Protestant and Pentecostal, but small children, young men and fathers. I don't think these are rigid categories, though it is possible to be a baby in one realm and a father in another; to have faith for miracles on the one hand, but to find a consistent walk of holiness and discipline hard on the other. But generally, our experience of God places us all at one of these levels.

If you're a baby in Christ, you know your sins are forgiven and you have come into a wonderful realization of God's Father-love towards you. You are vulnerable and weak, like a real baby, so God will feed you on spiritual milk and you will never find it so easy to receive from God.

A mother responds quickly to the cries of a newborn baby, and in the same manner Almighty God responds quickly to the cries of one of His new born! If you are a young man in Christ, you have begun to experience the power of God's Word in defeating the enemy. Instead of relying on your feelings God has been teaching you to live by His promises and to feed off the tree of life rather than knowledge. Consequently, it may be harder to appropriate your healing because God asks you to believe you have received your healing before you feel it. You believe what God says and not what your body is telling you. This doesn't mean going around saying, "I haven't got cancer, really, I've just got the symptoms," because you might as well say you have the real thing. We are not talking about mind over matter, but the authority of the Word of God.

If you are a father in the faith, you are not so much in the battle as in the victory. You know God not simply as Father, but as the Almighty One, the King and Creator. More than having a mere intellectual understanding of spiritual things, you have a deep knowledge of God Himself, of His thoughts and ways. If you have come to this point of maturity, you may be wasting your time asking someone to pray for you, because God may expect you to receive your healing through your communion faith with Him.

Let me give you three brief examples. I went to an Anglican church some years ago that was just on the brink of renewal. On the first evening, lots of people were baptized in the Spirit and spoke in tongues and on the second evening people began to manifest the spiritual gifts that they had never experienced before. Then on the third evening, an unsaved woman was carried into the church with a severely damaged back, hip, and leg. In the middle of preaching, I gave out a word which had suddenly come to me, "I believe God is going to heal someone right now to prove to them that Jesus Christ is Lord."

And straightaway she found she was healed, after years of agony from an incurable condition – not only wonderfully healed but also wonderfully saved.

On another occasion, I was in a Baptist church in the USA where I had to pray for the pastor who was in a steel corset because of a disintegrating spine. He had been filled with the Spirit for several years and was a mature Christian. I prayed for him and then said, "Brother, you are going to have to

106

act on your faith. Bend and touch your toes."

He looked at me as if I was mad, but after a few moments, he gingerly bent down – and discovered after he had obeyed God that there was no longer anything wrong with his back. He was overjoyed but I felt I should warn him that after a few days he might be challenged. (That isn't always the case; beware the theology which gets blessed for three days and expects the devil on the fourth! With that sort of faith, he is bound to pay a visit.)

But sure enough, four days later, I received a call and a weak voice said, "For three days my back has been wonderful, Ian, but now I am lying in bed and I can't move. What should I do?"

"Well, do you believe you are healed?" I asked. He mumbled into the phone, "Yes, I do."

So I asked the Lord what he should do and immediately into my mind flashed a sort of cartoon picture of him doing a somersault out of bed. "This will either kill or cure him," I thought, "I am glad that I have a travelling ministry."

"Well, brother," I announced, "God has shown me that you are to do a somersault out of bed."

There was a strangled gasp at the other end of the phone as he put the receiver on the table and there was a silence. Next I heard a thud and crash, and in a moment his breathless voice came on the telephone, "Oh brother, I wouldn't have believed it if I hadn't experienced it for myself, I am healed!"

He was a young man in the faith; he had been tested and had overcome;
He would not be tested on it again.

I know somebody who was involved in a car crash that seriously damaged his spinal column. As he lay semi-paralyzed in hospital, the Word of God came to him with a powerful anointing, "By His stripes, I was healed." In that moment he knew he had received his healing and over the next few days he lay there, still unable to move, speaking out what he knew in his heart, "By His stripes, I was healed." His testimony now is that for five days, his body told him he was paralyzed but at the end of that time he finally submitted to God's Word, and he was completely restored to strength. He was a "father" in the faith.

# Some Major Reasons why People are not Healed

In discussing the physical aspect of healing, we must remember that God's prime concern is wholeness. The Holy Spirit comes into our spirits at the new birth, restores our souls through many different dealings, and also quickens our mortal bodies. We know that God wants us to enjoy all His benefits, so what is wrong when people we pray for are not healed?

Sometimes we may feel full of faith, the anointing of God seems to be with us, and there is even a powerful sense of God's presence, yet the sickness remains. Most of us just withdraw and conclude that perhaps it wasn't God's time, or maybe it wasn't His will. Usually, though, we feel we have failed somehow, and the experience makes us reluctant to ask God why we have not received physical healing. I used to just accept that I didn't understand, but several years ago I felt I should seek God for specific reasons why some people are not healed, and He gave me eleven main ones.

It is not good enough to send people away with the old cliché "You do not have enough faith." If we have real love and compassion for people who are suffering, if we have genuine concern for the health of the Lord's body, we will give them support and encouragement; we will provide pastoral care and counselling for them and we will see them through into health, if we can.

Now I'm not suggesting that we should cross-examine people as if they were being interrogated. That can be unhelpful at best, and dangerously destructive at worst; it might lead people into introspection and condemnation. But with wisdom and discernment we can fit the right key into the lock and allow God's power to flow to them. In the course of our ministry we have experienced that the most common blockages that prevent healing taking place are:

## 1. Fear

Fear can present an obstacle to healing, and it may take several forms. Some people are afraid that if they trust themselves to God for healing and it doesn't work, they will lose what little relationship with Him they had at the start. Having been let down by others in the past, they fear being hurt by God in the same way, and so to protect their vulnerability, subconsciously they do not give themselves wholly to God. If they are able to receive His love, they can be set free from the fear of opening themselves up to Him.

For others, their deepest fear is the sickness itself, and ultimately, of death. They diagnose their symptoms as serious and do not even respond to assurances from the doctor that the complaint is minor. Some people are dominated by a fear of cancer and interpret every ailment as the "Big C." And others receive doctors' verdicts as death sentences, and are so afraid they are going to die that they cannot receive the word of life.

There are three ways of getting rid of fear. The first is to receive the peace of God through His Word:

> For God hath not given us a spirit of fear, but of power, of love and of a sound mind (2 Timothy 1:7, KJV).

To be honest, I find very often this alone does not work as the person is usually so bound with fear that he finds it impossible to respond to the Lord. In which case, it might be necessary to cast out a spirit of fear, and this may be successful unless, perhaps, the person is a very mature Christian! Then there isn't such a simple solution. Or, at least it is simple in a sense but it requires much more effort and self-denial, as this illustration shows.

While my wife and I were travelling and ministering in America, we arrived at the house of some good friends, feeling tired and looking forward to some rest and relaxation. It is often at these times that the devil seeks to attack our minds and our bodies. Rosemary recalls:

I was in the shower when I noticed a lump in my breast that took me by surprise. Could it be just a benign cyst or was it a malignant growth? Immediately a conflict began in my mind: God's Word versus the enemy's thoughts and fears. Pictures of hospitalisation, bouquets of flowers, even death suddenly loomed in my mind. At least I would become the centre of everyone's attention, but I also had thoughts of how my husband would cope without a wife and my child without mother. I decided this was no place to fantasize; this was reality. I had proved the healing power of Jesus before and He had never let me down, but now I needed living faith again. I decided to tell Ian that together we would stand against this attack on my body. We agreed together upon Matthew 18:19.

That night I lay down in bed but sleep did not come easily. I knew the truth of "by His stripes I was healed" and "Jesus Himself took all my infirmities and carried away my sickness" but I had to subject all my thoughts and Satan's lies to the Word of God. I began by thanking God for healing me nearly two thousand years ago and saying to myself, *"Surely goodness and mercy shall follow me all the days of my life"* (Psalm 23).

Then as I was focusing on Jesus, I heard Him speak to me. Just what I needed! He said, "I love you too much to let that deadly sickness happen to you." That settled it for me; God's breathed word was my final authority! I thanked the Lord and refused to think any other thoughts as I fell asleep. In the morning I refused to instinctively touch my body and feel for the lump in my breast. I did this consciously so that my senses would have no room to doubt, which allowed my faith to grow stronger. You can tell when you have overcome the crisis of faith because you no longer want to look at your body "to see" if you have been healed. You look because you know! We do not have to get rid of a physical problem, for as we receive the Word of God it becomes flesh in our experience and heals us. Jesus' stripes have paid the price for our healing and when we stop being occupied with our sicknesses, realize God's love for us, the Holy Spirit will bring to fruition what we believe.

After a week or so had passed I accidentally prodded myself where the lump had been and discovered that once more Jesus had triumphed; there was no sign of the lump. Faith in God's Word always works and brings results.

Rosemary's experience illustrates the third way to get rid of fear as found in Ephesians 5:20:

> ...always giving thanks to God the Father for everything, in the name of our Lord Jesus Christ.

We discussed the power of praise in a previous chapter and it really is the way out of the prison of fear. Many of us realize that applying it is much harder. We read:

> ...Wake up, O sleeper, rise from the dead and Christ will shine on you (Ephesians 5:14).

Most of us know that waking up does not present too much of a problem, but getting up is another matter. So it is with spiritual truths. After we have realized the truth of God's Word, we need to walk in it, and then Christ will give us revelation; we will see the fruit of our faith in our experience.

In the same passage, Paul goes on to say that we must "redeem the time" or make the most of every opportunity. Do not wait until your sickness is terminal before you seek prayer because time is against you: "the days are evil." At the first symptom, pray and go for ministry because if you leave it

110

and try the doctors, try the health food shop, try the chemists, by the time you get to God your condition may be desperate and you are terrified.

So if this is your problem, if you are full of fear and no one seems to have any answers or any hope, don't waste time wondering about the will of God. His will is stated clearly in the next verse in this passage:

> *...Be filled with the Spirit. Speak to one another with psalms, hymns and spiritual songs. Sing and make music in your heart to the Lord, always giving thanks to God the Father for everything, in the name of our Lord Jesus Christ* (Ephesians 5:18-20).

Proverbs 23:23 states that we should "buy" the truth, so there is a price to pay for walking in God's ways. It means denying your natural mind, or denying your feelings. It may hurt your pride. Praising God for your problem means dying a little, for it is only in losing your life that you come into His.

## 2. Misbelief

A misbelief is something you believe that has no foundation or truth. For instance a man might say, "I believe God has given me this illness like a thorn in the flesh to keep me humble."

Well, I would reply to him, "Really, brother? Fantastic! Let me sit at your feet."

He might not expect quite that reaction so I would explain to him that Paul had a thorn in the flesh and he wrote a large portion of the New Testament. Not only that, but the thorn, the messenger of Satan (probably a person, not a physical affliction anyway, but we won't go into that here) was sent to stop him from being too proud because he had been transported to Paradise and heard "inexpressible things," "surpassingly great revelations." So it would be fair to say that most of us don't qualify for a thorn at all.

Another misbelief is that "God is teaching us something through sickness." That may be a gracious by-product, but it is the Holy Spirit who is our teacher, not Satan, who is the author of all sickness. If we hold this misbelief, then when illness strikes, instead of taking authority over it and standing on our Calvary covenant, we will go into ourselves and start wondering "What is God showing me? What have I done wrong? What new revelation is God trying to give me?" By the time we find out, we might be almost dead because if we look inwards we will always find something wrong, and the devil will keep feeding us new problems. Nevertheless, we are told to look to Jesus. If we have this misbelief, we may never get to the point of being able to receive prayer, because we will never be sure if God has finished showing us all His deep truths.

I went to see some good friends in the United States when a bad flu bug was going around. The pastor's wife had been in bed for three or four weeks and was quite ill so I went along to see her. Going into her room, I said, "I've come to pray for you." But she didn't seem to hear.

"Oh, Ian," she cried, "I don't know what the Lord is saying in all this."

"Well, I believe Jesus' will is for you to be healed," I answered.

She responded, "I have not learned all He is trying to teach me yet."

I've heard other people say that their sickness is a sign from God that the church isn't walking right. Or, there is still sin in the body of Christ, and that their illness is a reflection of it. Yet there is no scriptural pattern for this thinking.

Someone else might say, "I've sinned, brother Ian, and God is burning the sin out of me." No, the devil pays his wages, and he is the most faithful employer in the world. The wage of sin is death, but the gift of God is eternal life through Jesus Christ, our Lord. God does not pay wages. He gives gifts. The devil makes people sick, but God sent Jesus to heal them.

A girl once came to me for prayer but insisted that she couldn't be healed as she had venereal disease.

"Why can't you be healed?" I asked. "Have you repented?"

"Oh yes," she replied, "years ago, but I can't be healed; it is incurable."

When I explained to her that God did not hold her past against her, and that once forgiven sin was forgotten by Him, and that Jesus had triumphed over the devil by dying and rising for us, I was able to pray for her and she was healed. Soon afterwards she conceived and gave birth to a beautiful, healthy baby, which was a miracle in itself.

To believe that your illness is inherited is another common misbelief. We touched before on the verses in Ezekiel 18:1-4:

*The Word of the Lord came to me:*
*"What do you mean by quoting the proverb about the land of Israel:*
*'The fathers eat sour grapes,*
*and the children's teeth are set on edge?'*
*As surely as I live," declares the Sovereign Lord, "you will no longer quote this*
*proverb in Israel."*

Now I know there is hereditary disease, but we should not regard it as a curse. If we think like this, we do away with the efficacy of the new birth; we deny the power that is in the blood of Jesus. We don't need healing but revelation, for Jesus took His blood up to heaven, presented it before His Father, and sprinkled it on the mercy seat of God. Moreover, the blood of Jesus speaks to God of better things than the cry of the law, or the blood of animals that was sprinkled on the mercy seat of the Old Covenant. That blood justifies me; I am born again by that blood. I am not who I thought I was! I may look the same, but inside I am a new creation. Therefore, I cannot inherit a disease from my parents because the old me has died. And I cannot blame my sickness on the sins of my family and ancestors because according to Ezekiel 18:4 every man dies for his own sins.

So-called hereditary illness is complicated by a double-barrelled fear. First, you are afraid you'll pass it on to your children, and that is an open door for a spirit of infirmity to get into them. Second, you are frightened that you can't be healed because it's not your problem but somebody else's, such as your grandfather or your mother. What we must realize, to break out of this fear, is that the devil is a master liar, and he insinuates the same disease in you as in your father. So the truth is you are not really inheriting a disease; rather, conjured by an evil spirit you manifest the same symptoms as your father 's affliction. If the devil has deceived you, he really has you because you will be praying for the wrong thing.

## 3. Scepticism and Unbelief

It is sad that there is such tremendous scepticism in the Body of Christ – "I'll believe it when I see it." Even when they do see it, they give all sorts of explanations why it might not be the work of God. If you are sceptical, God will never heal you. Jesus never wasted time on the sceptics; He just ignored them. For scepticism hides an "evil heart of unbelief" as the Bible puts it. It is the enemy of faith. Our problem is often not that we need more faith but that we need less unbelief so that our faith can work properly. Look at the episode in Mark 9 of the man who brought his epileptic son to the disciples for healing, but they were unable to drive out the evil spirit.

"Oh unbelieving generation," Jesus reproached them and turned to the father of the boy. Jesus could see that the disciples, confronted with the sight of such a serious affliction (the boy had been suffering from this violent condition from childhood and he was scarred from throwing himself into fire and water) were overwhelmed by their unbelief. Evidently, instead of admitting it, they attempted to pray for the boy even though they didn't really believe their prayers would work. Perhaps Jesus perceived in the boy's father a greater degree of openness and honesty; less pride too, possibly. He was desperate after all, and Jesus was now his only hope:

"If you can do anything, take pity on us and help us."

"If you can?" said Jesus. "Everything is possible for him who believes."

Straightaway the man saw what his problem was. Immediately the boy's father exclaimed, "I do believe; help me overcome my unbelief!"

His unbelief, nurtured every day by the terrible sight of his afflicted son, was preventing him from exercising his faith. Jesus confirms this, for in the same incident recorded by Matthew, after casting out the evil spirit with a single command, He tells His disciples why they have been unsuccessful:

> *"Because of your little faith. I tell you the truth, if you have faith as small as a mustard seed, you can say to this mountain, 'Move from here to there,' and it will move. Nothing will be impossible for you. But this kind does not go out except by prayer and fasting."*

This translation is rather confusing because on the one hand, Jesus rebukes them for only having little faith, and on the other, He says "faith as small as a mustard seed" is sufficient for great miracles. The point Jesus is making is that our faith need only be like the tiny mustard seed, which under the right conditions, grows at an amazing rate and reproduces prolifically, and the right conditions for our faith to grow like that is in the absence of the weeds of unbelief.

The only way to kill these weeds, Jesus says, is by prayer and fasting. I am convinced that "this kind" which He refers to is not the evil spirit but the disciples' unbelief. So when you fast and pray, you are not increasing your faith but getting rid of your unbelief, breaking the hold it has on your faith.

114

We read in Isaiah 58:6

> *'Is not this the kind of fasting I have chosen: to loose the chains of injustice and untie the cords of the yoke, to set the oppressed free and break every yoke?'*

Fasting breaks the yoke of your unbelief so that you are able to share what you have with those in need (v. 7) just like Peter and John with the crippled man at the Beautiful Gate. We speak the unhindered word of faith to bring life and healing:

> *Then your light will break forth like the dawn, and your healing will quickly appear...* (v. 8).

I remember a story recounted by a well-known preacher who went to Australia to speak in a number of meetings. In the healing time at the end of one service, a man came up to him for prayer, and this minister took one look at him, and said, *"I'm not going to pray for you, brother. You're full of unbelief. Go away, fast, and come back tomorrow."*

I should think the man was too astounded to argue but he went away and, sure enough, the next day he was there again in the healing line. Imagine his amazement when the preacher said, "Sorry, I'm not praying for you. You did not fast, did you?"

Red-faced, the man admitted he hadn't. Two nights later, and perhaps a couple of inches thinner, he stood before the preacher once more to be told, *"I do not need to pray for you now. You are healed already."* In that moment, he was.

## 4. Pride

The Bible says God opposes the proud (James 4:6) and will not walk with them. It is no good praying, "Lord, please humble me," because we are told to humble ourselves under the mighty hand of God. Some people are ashamed to admit they are sick because they feel it is an admission of failure and a lack of spirituality. This is pride, and if we have this attitude we cannot receive anything from God, for we believe we have achieved everything by our own efforts, and our present situation is due to our own weakness.

I discovered how full of pride I am through my own physical problem:
I stammer. Every time I felt out of my depth in a healing situation, I couldn't have stammered; if I tried; every time I felt very confident, I couldn't put two words together without tripping over them.

Pride can also infiltrate our motives in seeking healing. We say it is for the glory of God, but a part of us wants to be healed, or to pray for someone else's healing successfully, in order to prove our spirituality and to draw attention to ourselves. This is more likely to be a problem if we aren't too seriously sick. There is no leveller of pride like desperation.

## 5. Occult Involvement

There is absolutely no doubt that dabbling in the occult will hinder healing. Conscious and deliberate involvement in the works of darkness will certainly block God's power, but so also might unwitting participation in less obvious satanic practices – ouija boards, tarot cards, fortune telling, astrology, drugs, yoga, Transcendental Meditation, even some forms of alternative medicine. Repentance and renouncing of these involvements may remove the blockage straightaway, but unfortunately, they may have inflicted worse problems on ourselves than our sickness. We will certainly have exposed ourselves to demonic interference and we may need the ministry of deliverance; we may have actually jeopardized various areas of our lives, even be cursed. We see a graphic illustration in Isaiah 47:9-11:

> *Both of these will overtake you in a moment, on a single day: loss of* **children and widowhood.** *They will come upon you in full measure, in spite of your many sorceries and all your potent spells.*
>
> *You have trusted in your wickedness and have said, "No one sees me." Your wisdom and knowledge mislead you when you say to yourself, "I am, and there is none besides me."*
>
> *Disaster will come upon you, and you will not know how to conjure it away. A calamity will fall upon you that you cannot ward off with a ransom; a catastrophe you cannot foresee will suddenly come upon you* [emphasis added].

God loathes spiritism and occultism. He said, "You shall have no other gods before Me." By dabbling in the realms of darkness, we give Satan power and authority over us. Although he pretends to give with one hand so that we are lured into his kingdom, he robs us with the other yet so suddenly that we don't realize that he is the cause of our affliction. To illustrate, I have counselled so many women who have had one miscarriage after another. They have been prayed for that their wombs will be strengthened and that the pregnancy will be blessed, but still they lose their unborn children because of previous occult involvement.

116

In the firemen's strike in England some years ago, there was a tragic fire where in two little children died. There were horrific pictures of the children at the top of the house just before they were burned to death. Some months later, I was preaching Isaiah 47 in a nearby town (I had not understood then why the Lord had directed me to preach on this passage), and a woman broke down and came sobbing to the front of the meeting. She said she was the mother of the children who perished in the fire.

"I am a spiritist medium," she confessed through her sobbing, "and I cursed God for that fire, but now I see why it happened." She repented and God saved her that night, gloriously setting her free from all effects of her evil practices. Still, she had lost her two little children. There is a terrible price to pay for involvement in the occult.

Do not think that because you did not take the occult practice seriously, it didn't have any effect. It's rather like being exposed to radiation: you don't always see any outward sign, but deep inside, insidious damage is occurring, causing mutations in cells which may manifest as cancers many years hence. Even if you went to a fortune-teller once, just as a joke, beware. They tell you enough truth to catch you and then either you become dependent on them or you try to manipulate events and people to bring about or avoid what was foretold. You become dominated by curiosity or by fear. Either way, it is a curse, but Jesus gives us a promise of freedom and blessing.

## 6. Sin

If you practice sinful habits, you will probably have difficulty getting through to God, because if our heart condemns us, we have no confidence towards Him. Some people have a rather dull conscience, and it may be possible for them to relate to God and receive His blessings, but most of us do not expect to receive anything when we know we are disobeying and grieving God.

Never look inwards; look up at Jesus because when He convicts of sin, it is with His finger pointing specifically to the problem. When we are under the condemnation of the devil, we feel a heavy hand hitting us and crushing us. When God's Spirit points out our sin we know it is right because we have a witness inside, and since He shows it to us in the light of Calvary, we know we can confess our sin and be cleansed of it immediately, going on to receive our healing.

## 7. Despondency and Dismay

You have been prayed over many times, you have had more hands laid on you than you've had hot dinners, and still you are not healed. You cannot bear the thought of being prayed for again. Your despondency and dismay are understandable. The people of Israel must have felt the same as they stood at the entrance of the Promised Land at the beginning of the Book of Joshua. After forty years of wandering in the wilderness they hear that Moses, the great leader, the one they had always depended upon, has died. Fear, despondency, and dismay overwhelm them. After all they have been through, they feel too crushed by this last blow to overcome the final hurdle. They are on the point of giving up when the Word of the Lord comes to them through Joshua:

> ...*Now then, you and all these people, get ready to cross the Jordan River into the land I am about to give to them – to the Israelites. I will give you every place where you set your foot as I promised Moses... No one will be able to stand up against you all the days of your life. As I was with Moses, so I will be with you; I will never leave you nor forsake you.*
>
> **Be strong and courageous**, *because you will lead these people to inherit the land I swore to their forefathers to give them.*
>
> **Be strong and very courageous.** *Be careful to obey all the law my servant Moses gave you; do not turn from it to the right or to the left, that you may be successful wherever you go. Do not let this Book of the Law depart from your mouth; meditate on it day and night, so that you may be careful to do everything written in it. Then you will be prosperous and successful. Have I not commanded you?* **Be strong and courageous. Do not be terrified; do not be discouraged, for the Lord your God will be with you wherever you go"** (Joshua 1:2-9 [emphasis added]).

Three times God says "be strong and courageous." There is no way out. God tells us, if we want to go into the Promised Land, we must put some steel in our will and act like the victors, not the vanquished.

Repeatedly through the New Testament, there echoes the cry "**stand firm, and having done all, stand.**" The idea of the world is, if you cannot cope with life, turn to religion. If you cannot succeed at any other job, become a minister! What a reputation. Obviously the church will – and should – bring in the lost, the weak, and the needy, but once they have made Jesus Christ their Lord, the weak hands and feeble knees ought to be strengthened.

Whatever we say about life not being a bed of roses, as Christians, many of us still do not expect to have to fight for anything, as if there wasn't a devil trying to rob, usurp, and destroy us. God promises to be with us every step of the way so when things don't work out, why not get aggressive with the devil and refuse to give up? We need to get righteously angry about the territory the devil has stolen from the church. When we get some spiritual adrenaline going, we start fighting and it's the despondency and dismay that are put to flight. Resist the devil and he will flee from you.

## 8. Self-Pity

Poor me. Why is life always so hard for me? Why should I be the one to suffer all this pain? Unfortunately, it's only a short step from there to the accusation, "God, why did You allow this to happen to me?" Then we find we are letting in anger, resentment, and all their attendant problems. On the other hand, we simply become so absorbed by our own condition, obsessed by our symptoms, that we actually start to enjoy our illness in a morbid sort of way.

In the early days of my ministry, when I became ill, I would come home and be sick there. After all, it wouldn't look good to be sick while I was out preaching about healing. In fact, I was usually healthy on the road because as long as I was preaching healing, I lived in it. But when I stopped, I would let my guard down and the devil would make me sick. When I got safely home, I would decide I was really sick and would rationalize I deserved a day in bed anyway. My wife would ask, "Shall I call the elders?" and I would hastily say we shouldn't bother them as they were so busy.

"Just draw back the curtains, darling, so that I can see the sunshine, (lying back feebly on my pillows), and do not let anyone come around today. I need some peace and quiet."

It didn't seem so bad to be sick after all, and just as my wife was going out of the bedroom, I would say: "Darling, I've just had a vision. I see a lunch tray with…" By this time, her patience would have run out, the bedclothes would be on the floor, and I would be exercising my faith or dying of pneumonia.

I remember the first time I preached about healing. I awoke the next morning with the most violent stomach pains I have ever had in my life. I thought I was dying. "It's not fair," I groaned. "I didn't mean to attack the devil like that. What sort of reward is this for preaching the Word?"

Rosemary, my wife, wasn't exactly sympathetic, however.

'Get up,' she said.

So up I got and staggered round the bedroom, muttering, "By His stripes, I was healed. By His stripes, I was healed."

God let me walk around that wretched floor for forty-five minutes and then He spoke to me:

"Do you believe that by My stripes, you were healed?" "Yes Lord," I said.

"Well stop trying to get healed then."

As I relaxed and looked to Him, I was healed, just like that.

"Lord." I protested, "Why did you wait for forty-five minutes?"

"I was just bringing a little death to self-pity." He replied.

"I could have healed you the minute you got out of bed, but you were so full of self-pity that it was more important to get rid of some of that first."

Three quarters of an hour walking around in agony shows that God meant business as much as I did – though I was about to get back into bed so maybe that's why God thought He had better give me a victory! However, He hates self-pity because that's when we put ourselves on the throne, at the centre of the world. We consider ourselves instead of denying ourselves; we push God out.

## 9. Apathy

I believe apathy is one of the major demonic principalities in the world. Over so many things, people say they are not bothered, they don't care. There is no sense of urgency about most of what we do. Bored or dissatisfied with our lot, we still haven't got the energy or inclination to do anything about it. Moreover, this apathy has infiltrated the church too. When people come forward for healing, I sometimes ask them a few questions: Have you prayed for yourself? No. Have you fasted? No. Have you sought God with all your heart? No. Have you read the Bible this month? No. Have you been to church this week? No. What have you come for? Healing. Do you really want to be healed? Well no, actually it's rather nice being off work. People seldom admit this, of course, but you can tell by the shifty look and the change of subject that this is the real answer. It's hard work, being healthy. Have you ever reflected that living in health means never taking another day off from work? Most of us enjoy a good lie in, and we lie wallowing on beds of self-pity, fear, dismay, misbelief…

Jesus healed many people who were carried to Him on stretchers, or lying helpless on the ground. His command was not "be healed," but "rise up," "stand," "take up your bed and walk." He knows that before they could physically walk, their spirits had to rise up first. No wonder Jesus said to the man lying by the pool of Bethesda, who had been ill for thirty-eight years, "Do you want to get well?" (John 5:6). What is behind the man's answer?

> *"Sir, the invalid replied, I have no one to help me into the pool when the water is stirred. While I am trying to get in, someone else goes down ahead of me" (v. 7).*

Notice the man does not reply directly to Jesus' question. He seems keen to make excuses, to put the blame on other people, but there seems a certain amount of self-pity and probably laziness too. If he were healed, he would have to leave his security (he must have been quite a local personality if he had been lying there for thirty-eight years), leave the money he received from begging for alms, and face the difficulty of trying to find work and earn his keep after a lifetime of dependence. Jesus gives him the short, sharp, shock treatment: "Get up! Pick up your mat and walk."

That's not the tone you generally use to someone who has been earnestly, whole-heartedly, courageously seeking healing for years. I think the man leapt up as if he had been stung. He was healed the moment Jesus spoke but he would not have known it until he made the effort to get up. Jesus reprimanding him slightly is borne out by His comment.

He finds him at the temple later that day: "See, you are well again. Stop sinning, or something worse may happen to you" (v. 14).

Now a man who has been crippled for thirty-eight years does not have much scope for active sin. But Jesus could see his thoughts and warned him against the apathy which had kept him an invalid for so long.

## 10. Rebellion, Resentment, and Anger

I have treated these as one since generally all three are present at the same time. We are all aware that there are various streams, denominations, fellowships, and other groups that make up the Body of Christ around the world. Sometimes these different fellowships co-exist quite happily, but there are many sad examples of rebellion, criticism, and hurt, which cause great stumbling blocks to the spiritual growth of the individuals and fellowships involved.

If I minister to a group that has broken away, I encourage it to pray to make sure there is no rebellion in the hearts of its members. It may have been that God desired the break in order to do something different with them or simply to bring growth, since most organisms grow by cell division. But occasionally the split was because of personality clashes, because certain individuals found it impossible to submit to the leadership of the church, or because the elders have refused to delegate responsibility or accept new ideas. A lot of hurts happen in these situations. I usually ask the group to pray in tongues, thinking of the leadership which asked them to leave, and to keep on praying in tongues until they have nothing but love in their hearts for those concerned. You can never build if there is rebellion in the camp. The group will split and splinter again.

Obviously, the list of blockages to healing is not exhaustive; one or two others were mentioned earlier in the book, and doubtless you will be able to think of more. But one final problem is so pervasive and profound that it needs a chapter of its own to discuss it fully; that problem is rejection.

# Rejection and an Orphan Spirit

In 1976, Rosemary and I bought a lovely old thatched cottage in Chard, England. At least, it was potentially lovely, but it needed complete renovation.

I would have been happy just to repaint the walls, but I saw Rosemary with that gleam in her eye, which meant she intended "a total renovation," so we did. After soaking the wall, we peeled off the paper to find another layer underneath, so we scrubbed away at that, only to find another floral creation underneath, and another, and another. We went through about five layers before the plaster finally fell away under the strain. And if God hadn't spoken to me then, I would not have felt like speaking to Rosemary for months:

"That's what I'm doing to people's lives," He said. "I'm not interested in just patching something up. I'm pulling it all down until we reach the solid rock. And that's what I'm doing in your life. The day you asked Me to heal you, I started."

"It doesn't look much like it, Lord," I replied darkly.

"But remember Jeremiah," was His reply. "I told him to uproot and tear down, to destroy and overthrow, and then to build and plant. Its taken all these years to clear the ground before I can sow and build."

So that was what He had been doing. I wish He had told me. I had spent years struggling through doubt, fear, insecurity, and anger because I had interpreted all that happened as God not caring, rather than God loving me. Through this incident, He started to show me what was at the root of all my sense of failure and hurt. Rejection. And I am convinced, years later, that this is the main reason why some people do not receive their healing.

Why should rejection be such a common problem? I think there are several reasons. First, people of my age are paying the price of World War II or the corporate demands on parents. For so many children, their father was away for extended periods of time, either serving their country or their bosses. Second, with a divorce rate of at least one in three (higher in the United States), the family structure is breaking down. Children are growing up in an atmosphere of insecurity without models of faithfulness, loyalty, and morality on which to base their own lives. Third, our culture frowns upon public display of emotion or affection. Our private school system has perpetuated this so that many adult relationships of people with that upbringing suffer through a difficulty in expressing feelings. A lack of communication breeds hurt, insecurity and rejection. Fourth, more and more children are being brought up by secondary care givers or left at playgroups and nurseries all day while mothers work. Whatever the reasons for this situation, it is a sad fact that many children lack a sense of stability and reassurance, as insufficient attention and love is given to them to build up their self-esteem. The list goes on.

I was born in 1939, the first of two children, and my impression during the first six years of my life was, "My father doesn't love me." He seemed to be always busy or away from home, and when I did see him he was pre-occupied with his own problems. I wasn't badly treated or neglected physically, but such a lack of affirmation and attention made me grow up feeling very rejected. For I do believe that it is the father who moulds the emotional life of the child. A mother's love is natural and instinctive; there is normally an immediate bond between mother and child at birth. But a father who loves his child is able to develop it to the fullness of its ability. He will encourage the child to help him tend the yard. He will take an interest in the games, projects, and hobbies. He will spend time just talking and encouraging. He will build up the child's self-respect, confidence, and security. He will be there for a hug and a cuddle, as a counsellor and a shoulder to cry upon.

My own reaction to the absence of all these benefits was made more negative through my school and church experiences. Handicapped with a terrible stutter, I vividly remember being told impatiently by a teacher at the age of seven, "It's no good asking you for the answer, we will be waiting ten minutes for it to come."

She might as well have taken a stick and caned me – in fact that might not have damaged me as much. At children's Sunday school, I was taught that we were made in the image of God. The idea amazed me looking at my terrible stuttering problem.

The irony of the situation was that inside I had plenty of willpower and ambition. My heart's desire was to be an attorney, and in my mind's eye I could see myself standing in court dazzling everyone by my brilliance. I could use words powerfully and I thought I would make a marvellous prosecutor, wringing confessions out of sobbing defendants with my blistering attacks. The only time I did not stutter was when I was angry. Part of me, too, wanted to be an actor, which I think stemmed from a desire to escape from

124

all my failings and inhibitions and win admiration and praise. In reality, of course, I could not put two words together without falling over them, and everyone said I wasting my time thinking about the legal profession. In the end, I settled for accountancy, but this compromise only increased the chip on my shoulder; I felt that life (or God?) had treated me badly.

One day I decided that I had had enough. I started fasting and I meant to fast until "You heal me, Lord, and if You don't, they can inscribe on my tombstone that I died trying to get healed." But after several days, God managed to make me see that I was not truly fasting. I was on a hunger strike. Then He spoke to me very clearly: "I have called you to preach the gospel and heal the sick."

I should have been overwhelmed, thrilled, excited, and grateful at such a promise. But to be honest it didn't please me at all. The last thing I wanted was a healing ministry. Whoever heard of a preacher with a stammer? It sounded like a rather sick joke. But maybe I could do some bargaining.

"Heal me first, and I'll go."

The answer came like the slam of a prison door:

"No, go as you are, and everyone will know who the healer is."

"That's not fair, Lord," I protested.

"If you want what is fair, you can go to hell," the Lord replied. You can't argue with that.

There followed a gruelling year that became a training ground for my emerging healing ministry. For the first six months I was unemployed, and then the church encouraged us to walk in faith and trust the Lord to support us. Live by faith!

I can see, with hindsight, that even though I was hearing from God about my calling there was undoubtedly a spirit of rejection that acted as a filter, distorting to my ears what should have been an honour and a blessing. I was being robbed by that spirit because it influenced all my emotions of insecurity and prevented me from fully trusting God in faith.

This spiritual interference was present throughout many years of fruitful ministry and was used to lessen my expectation, cut off opportunities, distort my picture of God in my personal life, and prevent my faith from working fully and being a blessing to me personally.

Many people who come for healing have been prayed for many times previously. They now almost have faith to be rejected yet again, as this insidious spirit has distorted their ability to both see and receive. We must recognize its work and cast it out before the person is able to receive their healing from God. Satan is called the father of lies, and his goal is to corrupt our idea of God's nature as a father who loves His children, and the spirit of rejection is one of his major tools for carrying out this work.

Many people in the churches have suffered from this problem for so long it has become their second nature. Often, they are reluctant to submit to leadership as their trust factor has been destroyed through situations in the past. Often the leadership mistake this lack of trust for rebellion, but that is putting the axe to the branch of the tree and not, as Jesus said, to the root of the tree. Many church leadership teams have their effectiveness and vision thwarted because one or more members are troubled by this spirit.

Rejection started in the Garden of Eden and once it enters a family, it will quickly become dysfunctional. If anyone suffers emotional, physical, or sexual abuse, they will almost certainly need to receive prayer to be set free of rejection as well as other problems. Once its presence is recognized, it will often appear like a python that has wound its way through the whole body. This spirit is frequently responsible for causing physical illness, and when praying against either cancer or diabetes, it is wise to ask the person whether there has been a specific event or a history of rejection in their experience, as our ministry experience has often discerned rejection as the main source. When this spirit has been dealt with, the symptoms of the illness frequently disappear, resulting in a return to health.

If this issue is not settled, all your relationships will be marred. You may have lots of friends and colleagues but find that they do not last. This may be because, subconsciously, you believe that rejection will raise its ugly head eventually. Instead of your faith working for you and with you, it will appear twisted and work negatively against you.

Rejection has a companion called an orphan spirit or orphan heart. This enters when some primary emotional need is not met within a family unit. We need to keep this in mind, on the occasions when prayer against rejection issues does not solve the problem. Like a real weak-willed orphan with deep emotional needs that can never be satisfied, so it is in the realm of the spirit

126

with a constant need for approval and an insatiable desire for greater and greater experiences which never seem to be enough.

For many years of my ministry, rejection and orphan spirit robbed me of confidence, joy, and blessing. This was partly due to my stuttering problem, but also because of the influence of these demonic forces which vexed my spirit.

I recall the day. I had been set apart for the work of the ministry. I had been called by the Lord, commissioned, ordained, and sent out by the elders of the church. Instead of being confident, happy, and expectant of the miracles God would perform, I was nervous and very frightened. My first task was simple: drive a church minister to the airport and then chauffeur a lady to the home of her friend. Upon arrival at the friend's home, I was invited in for refreshments before heading off to my first preaching engagement. The simple, polite conversation seemed to me a major interrogation, so I became nervous and I started to stutter very severely. My hosts were unnerved, and they suggested we pray. It was during this time – for the first time – that God broke into my conscious mind. "One of these ladies has a kidney problem." I panicked instead of thinking, "That is wonderful, Lord, now I am going to see a miracle; but suppose that is wrong? I will look foolish." I stammered the information and one of the ladies, a Catholic, acknowledged her condition. I prayed, but did not really expect anything to happen. I did not know how to pray and so I prayed for a long time, hoping the moment would never pass. I finally opened my eyes and saw the lady I had prayed over lying very still on the floor. I should have rejoiced and worshipped that God had obviously moved powerfully on her, but I was paralyzed. I was very afraid that she had died and that I was in serious trouble!

A few weeks later, I received a letter from the lady informing me that at that time, she had only about one week to live. She had been to Lourdes and also to Rome to get healed without success, but when I prayed for her, God totally healed her. Any normal person would have broken out in praise and worship to God for His faithfulness, but because of the rejection issues in my life, I was relieved just to hear from her at all.

So this was my first experience of healing. Soon afterwards, Rosemary, the baby, and I went off to Sweden to minister as someone in our church had some contacts there. We stayed there for about three months, mainly because we could not afford to come home again!

For several more years, it seemed as if we struggled on living on the knife edge of bankruptcy, and although the Lord was doing some amazing things at the meetings where I spoke, I still had no assurance of His love and leading. Every time I got up to preach I would be terrified that the Holy Spirit wouldn't turn up; hundreds of people would get healed and I would ask them, "Are you sure you're healed? Haven't you even got just a bit of pain left?" I was constantly hounded by feelings of anxiety and fear, and I think, deep down, I felt that my calling was a sentence, not a gift.

To make things worse, on several occasions when we arrived home from our travels, we found that the people who had been living in our home had left us a damaged kitchen, dirty carpets, or smashed china. Rosemary, as usual, was able to praise God through all this, but it didn't do anything for my sense of rejection and anger.

In 1976, I was invited to speak at a retreat centre in Canada for French-speaking Roman Catholics. I dreaded it. How did I manage to get myself into this situation? With my church background, they were bound to reject me, and anyway, I was still stuttering badly. What could I say to them to gain their sympathy? How about the Virgin Mary? That was bound to bless them.

I had been asked to come along at four o'clock in the afternoon to pray for the sick in a hospital wing of the convent. As I looked at the chronically sick, I felt my faith sink to my boots; I prayed for them then, but in my heart I knew that it was beyond me to pray the prayers of faith.

I left hurriedly, not waiting to see the response to my prayers. In the church, we waited in vain for the interpreter to show up. After a few minutes of preaching in monosyllabic English, I realized that my idea of the Virgin Mary was rather different, and the more I spoke, the bigger hole I dug for myself. I had dug a grave in about twenty minutes, so the priest stood up and gave a benediction that put us all out of our miseries. Just as he did, God gave me a three-dimensional vision, as vivid and as real as the congregation in front of me. Suddenly I saw a man in the hospital lying under a white sheet, which I assumed was an oxygen tent because I had never seen one, and I knew he had three coronaries and God had healed him. I did not know how to respond because the meeting was closing, but I walked over to the priest and said, "Excuse me, Father, but I have a vision."

The poor man looked rather vexed, and muttered something about this being highly irregular after the benediction, but to his credit, he asked if I would like to share it with the congregation. It seemed to me I had very little credibility left to lose so I might as well do so, and if it were right, God would get the glory. So when the priest had everyone's attention again, I described what I saw.

Instantly, two French-speaking nuns grabbed tambourines and started to jump up and down, praising God and crying, "That's Mr. So-and-So we been praying for!" "Hallelujah." I thought, "It looks like something happened anyway, but I'm not staying to find out."

The next day I returned as planned to England, but I was still angry and bitter towards God, – hurt and rejected by the way He seemed to have let me down and then humiliated me, first at the hospital wing of the convent, and then in the meeting where I had to preach. When I got home I found a convention on the theme of God's love in progress. It seemed the final twist of God's peculiar sense of humour and, unable to bear it any more, I stood up in front of everyone and said:

"If God loves me, He has a very funny way of showing it. I have been asking Him for many years to heal me, and I thought He promised to do it if I preached and did His will. Quite honestly, I might as well throw the whole thing in."

Dead silence. Everyone looked away, embarrassed. I turned around and walked out.

Next day, the pastor called and he got right to the point. "The trouble with you," he said, "is that you only know in your mind and not in your soul that God loves you."

No prizes for stating the obvious, but in fact if you had asked me if I thought God loved me, I would have said, "Of course."

"You believe He will bless everyone else," he continued, "that's why you're happy to minister to the sick; but you don't believe He is concerned about you. You can't really trust Him or receive anything from Him. What you have is a spirit of rejection."

He said a lot more that seemed to open me up like a surgeon's knife, cutting right through to the problem; and then he prayed for me. I was gloriously released from my anger and sense of rejection and for the first time in my life, I began to feel God's personal love for me.

Several weeks later, I got a letter from Canada:

> Dear Rev. Andrews,
> Last time you visited Canada, someone was raised from the dead. We would like you to come and talk about it on T.V. and radio...

I replied dryly that if someone had been raised from the dead I would have remembered it, that there was obviously some mistake. Perhaps they meant Brother Andrew from Holland? Then about two weeks later, I got another letter from a church saying the same thing, asking me to go over to Canada and speak. I decided I would have to go and see about all the confusion.

I was amazed to discover that the man I had seen in the vision had, in fact, been lying dead under a sheet. Suddenly he sat upright and started speaking in tongues, so the hospital sent him home. Now his next-door neighbours had just heard he had died, so they were somewhat surprised to see him tending his yard! The news spread like wildfire, and quite a Catholic community started up through that one healing. The Catholic Retreat Centre asked me to come back to speak to them, and that would have been fine, except that once more I was asked (groan) to pray for the sick in the hospital wing. When I arrived at four o'clock, I was immediately handed a cup of tea, shown to a chair and treated like an honoured guest. Then reality hit when they asked me to come to the ward again. But when we got there, I could hardly see an occupied bed. Apparently, almost everyone had been healed on my last visit! By this time, I felt I was in a dream, and when six hundred people turned up at the meeting that night, and dozens received salvation and healing, I was past the point of surprise. Maybe God does care after all.

From Canada, I went down to speak on a TV chat show in front of several million viewers in Chicago. Part of me would have loved that public opportunity to speak, but the rest of me was absolutely terrified. With my speech problem, I was bound to look ridiculous and any doors that were opening up for me would surely shut quickly. In fact, it rubbed on a sore spot because I felt God was making a fool of me again, so I rebelled against it and decided, as it was a cold winter, the best way out was to pray for snow so that I couldn't make it to the studio. (It started snowing the moment the program finished and stopped five days and fifteen feet later!)

There was no way out, so I presented myself at the studio like a man going to an execution. I was made up, and then told that when my cue came, I should run down the steps, sit in the chair, and say "Praise God!" Now the chat show was going out live, and I was to be the guest from 9:30 to 11:00 A.M. Unfortunately, no one had told the host that I stuttered. I ran down the stairs, managed not to fall over, the cameras zoomed in on me, and fear hit me like a bullet, and I burbled: "Pppppppr."

The interviewer gaped and made frantic signs for the camera to swing on to him.

130

"Mr. Andrews, I gather you have spoken at a conference of twenty-five thousand people and there have been some spectacular healings. Would you like to tell us what is happening there?"

The cameras came back to me, and I was still trying to respond.

The first few minutes were a nightmare. I think both of us wished that the floor would open up and swallow us. I felt as if God had completely deserted me, and in desperation I cried out to Him, "God, please do something!" From that moment, I couldn't have stammered if I tried. The anointing came down and I began to speak fluently and confidently.

My host hardly knew what to make of it. For the rest of the program I was able to testify to His power and love without any hesitation.

As soon as we came off the air, I was still devastated by that sense of abandonment and humiliation at the beginning of the program. I went back to my hotel room, laid on the floor, and felt a tide of rejection flow over me again. I couldn't pray, I wondered how I could possibly carry on ministering, and all my faith for healing seemed to have gone. I didn't expect to hear from God, but nevertheless through all my hurt came His voice with an extraordinary message.

"You are going to meet someone with an orphan spirit."

A what? I had never heard of such a thing, and anyway, what an irrelevant thing to say at a time like this. Still, I couldn't be bothered even to question it.

The next day I travelled on to another church. I had been invited to stay in the pastor's home, and as I walked in the door, his wife took one look at me and broke down and wept. It was as if a tap had been turned on. I have provoked strange reactions in the past, but no one has ever burst into tears after one glance! Without my saying a word, she poured out her story, telling me her father had just died, but she was glad he was dead because he had beaten her repeatedly as a child if she wasn't perfectly behaved, and she had hated him all her life. "And the last thing I want to hear from you," she sobbed bitterly, "is that God loves me and wants to be my Father."

Instantly, God spoke to me: "There's your orphan spirit."

It can't be, Lord, she had a father.

"So do orphans," God replied, "but she has never been fathered. And neither have you."

This was all too much at once. It was late, and I suggested that we shelve it for the night and talk the next morning. In the meantime, I knew I had some business with God.

As I laid in bed that night, God began to speak right into my heart.

"You know My lordship, but you don't know My fatherhood. Your prayers for others are answered but how many prayers for yourself are?"

The Lord was putting His hand on the very centre of my deepest wound. All these years in the ministry and I had never had confidence at all that God would look after us. It was Rosemary whose faith had kept us alive; she who prayed for money to pay the mortgage, the washing machine to be mended, for bills to be met. I remembered how I was told after I was baptized in the Spirit that I should pray to the Father rather than to Jesus. But this had created a negative situation for me, because my concept of our heavenly Father was based on my earthly one, and God consequently appeared to me as someone who was too busy and remote to have time for me.

That night, as I laid all these things before the Lord, confessed them, and asked for His deliverance and healing, I was wonderfully set free from that orphan spirit. The next morning, in the light of what had happened, the pastor prayed with me that any vacuum left by the orphan spirit would be filled with God's Holy Spirit of "adoption" or "sonship" (Romans 8:15) by which we cry "Abba, Father."

As he prayed over me, I knew as I had never done before that I was God's child and that He loved me as His son, for I seemed to feel Him put His arms around me and say, "Son, I love you." A sense of security and peace filled me. From that day, I have never had a trace of nervousness when I get up to speak, and my stammer has disappeared except for the odd hesitation, but this doesn't bother me as I know my Father loves me.

What happened to me was what Paul described:

> *I pray that out of his glorious riches he may strengthen you with power through his Spirit in your inner being so that Christ may dwell in your hearts through faith. And I pray that you, being rooted and established in love, may have power, together with all the saints, to grasp how wide and long and high and deep is the*

*love of Christ, and to know this love that surpasses knowledge – that you may be filled to the measure of all the fullness of God* (Ephesians 3:16-19).

We then prayed together for the pastor's wife together and she too was delivered of the orphan spirit and came into a glorious experience of God's fatherly love. With this wonderful revelation, I went into the church meeting to preach. At the end a girl with a disfiguring harelip and cleft palate stood up. She explained that she had never had faith for healing before but today she had a glimmer of hope. Then she broke down in tears, and tragically described the way her father had always refused to walk beside her as a child because he was embarrassed by the way she looked. Her sense of hurt and rejection was obvious. I explained to her that first she had to forgive her father for the way he had treated her. This she did, and then I prayed for her.

The next day, at a larger meeting, I was preaching on "by His stripes, we are healed," and again this girl stood up in front of the congregation and simply said, "Look what God has done to my mouth." The harelip had closed over, the cleft palate had disappeared and she stood laughing through her tears – a beautiful young woman. Apparently for years, people had prayed for her unsuccessfully and had assumed it was her lack of faith, but in fact, the blockage had been in her because she felt she wasn't pretty enough, good enough, worthy enough. She had never known a father's love.

That evening, I spoke about what God had revealed to me through my own healing experience. He had shown me that there were three degrees of knowing God's love:

1. Because the Bible tells me so.
2. Because He answers my prayers.
3. Because I feel Him loving me.

Suddenly a girl at the back of the church started to scream and cry, stumbling forward where I stood. By the time she reached the front, her makeup was smeared all over her face, and she was a pitiful sight. Oblivious of everyone else, she explained that she was a prostitute, and as she walked past the church that evening, trying to pick up a client, she suddenly heard a voice that said "Come In."

Not knowing what she was really doing, she opened the door and was riveted by what I was saying about God's love. It seemed as if God was speaking specifically to her. A hater of men and God, she told a horrific story of how her father had committed incest with her at an early age.

Emotionally damaged, she was later seduced by a church pastor at the age of fourteen. Turning to another church, the choir leader impregnated her at the age of eighteen and she had an abortion. From then until now, at the age of twenty-three, she had wanted to destroy men and that was why she had become a prostitute. All this was said over the loudspeakers, so caught up was she in her pain and anger. Gently, I explained that God could heal all those scars and give her a new life if she would first forgive her father, the minister, and the choir leader. There was a long pause and I watched her dig her sharp, painted nails into the palm of her hand. Then, through gritted teeth, she muttered, "I forgive them." Instantly, the power of God knocked her to the floor. After a few minutes, she jumped up, and with all the joy and openness of a young child, she gave me a big hug. Three or four years later, I heard that she married and became wonderfully settled with a secure home and children.

A day or two later, I flew home with a new appreciation of the importance of parents, particularly fathers, to give a sense of security and worth to their children. So when my son Stephen said to me rather wistfully, "Couldn't we spend some time together, Dad?" I did not give him the usual "I am too busy" brush off. Instead we sat down together and discussed what he would most like to do.

"Golf," he replied without hesitation.

"Great," I agreed, wondering how we could afford it. Doing an accountant's lightning calculation, I realized it would cost us about £500 to join the local golf club and get us both fitted out with clubs and bags. And we had literally not a penny in the bank. That night I prayed with a new confidence that God would provide us with the money to join the club and buy our equipment. The next day a check arrived from a London church for £500, with a note saying: "for private use."

Since all this happened, I have found that the main reason why people are not healed is rejection or an orphan spirit. Rejection stems from a broken relationship within or outside the family; an orphan spirit is the result of a breakdown between parent and child. In both cases, the path to healing starts with repentance and forgiveness because there is nearly always resentment and anger underneath the hurt.

Some years ago, while speaking in the north of England, a woman with a terminal illness suddenly interrupted me angrily, "I have come here because I was told it was a healing service so why are you going on about rejection?"

I explained that she would see the relevance if she listened a little longer, and she subsided into her seat, only to leap up a little while later, this time in tears.

"My husband left me for a younger woman eighteen months ago when I was fifty-two," she wept. "When I looked in the mirror, I hated myself and I hated him."

Six months later, she developed breast cancer and had radical surgery. Her resentment grew. Six months after that, a tumour developed in her other breast, then secondaries elsewhere. She knew that she was dying but she did not care. No one loved her anyway. But now she said without prompting, "I know I have to forgive him."

And she did. Like the others, she fell to the ground under the power of the Holy Spirit and when she stood up, all pain had disappeared.

(Incidentally, in case you think people fall on the floor every time I pray for them, as far as I am concerned, it's fine when it happens, but I don't necessarily expect it or encourage it. But with rejection it does seem to be a common occurrence, as if this is such a deep hurt that often only deep surgery under the anaesthetic of the Holy Spirit is the channel through which God's healing can flow.)

One of the saddest things about rejection is the person's bitter regret for the wasted years of childhood or marriage; the time is gone and can never be redeemed. Not only were those years diseased and bitter, but they blighted all future relationships and events. But God gives hope and a glorious promise:

> *I will restore to you the years that the swarming locust has eaten, the hopper, the destroyer, and the cutter, my great army, which I sent among you. You shall eat in plenty and be satisfied and praise the name of the Lord your God, who has dealt wondrously with you. And my people shall never again be put to shame* (Joel 2:25-26, EVS).

All those years are not lost and wasted forever! God will not only heal the effects of those early hurts but He will redeem the time, give you back the joy, the security, and the love you thought you could never know. Never again will you have to feel ashamed. Never again will you consider yourself worthless, or unlovable; for God has made you His child. He dwells inside you by His Spirit so that you can call Him Abba, Daddy, and you have the identity and security of belonging to His family forever. This was the wonderful revelation Jesus brought that God was no longer the unapproachable El Shaddai, God Almighty, but our Father. Hallowed be His name!

# God's Government in Healing

The Corinthian church was wonderfully blessed with spiritual gifts. People were saved, healed, delivered, preaching, prophesying, teaching, working miracles, healing the sick, speaking in tongues…there was a lot of enthusiasm and there were many spectacular happenings. But maybe there was also a bit of confusion and fear, even envy and criticism. As young Christians, they all needed some guidelines how to exercise their spiritual gifts, and in 1 Corinthians 12, Paul gives some basic teaching on the purpose of these gifts and their importance in the context of the body of Christ, in particular, the local community of believers. Paul is very concerned that there should be neither pride nor inferiority, emphasizing that a body is made up of many parts, that even the most insignificant member was of vital importance to the whole. But he also sees the importance of these parts working in harmony, with the body taking its orders from the head.

> *There are different kinds of gifts, but the same Spirit. There are different kinds of service, but the same Lord. There are different kinds of working, but the same God works all of them in all men.*
>
> *Now to each one is the manifestation of the Spirit given for the common good*
> (1 Corinthians 12:4-7).

There is a whole variety of gifts, service and working, so how can all these be brought together into some sort of order? In Isaiah 9:6, we read an interesting verse:

> *…And the government will be on his shoulders…*

Where are the shoulders? On the body. So the government of God's kingdom will be in the body of Christ, in the church. The church will provide a Spirit-inspired administration of God's gifts. The rest of the chapter is devoted to the operation of this governing structure.

> *Now you are the body of Christ, and each one of you is a part of it. And in the church, God has appointed first of all apostles, second prophets, third teachers, then workers of miracles, also those having gifts of healing, those able to help others, those with gifts of administration, and those speaking in different kinds of tongues* (1 Corinthians 12:27-28).

Now verse 29 is crucial: "Are all apostles?"

The answer is clearly

No.

"Are all prophets?"

 No.

"Are all teachers?"

No.

"Do all work miracles?"

No.

"Do all have gifts of healing?"

Following Paul's logical argument, the answer must again be No. Is Paul suggesting then, that only some people can pray for the sick? Well, yes and no! First of all, Paul seems to be making a distinction between ministries and gifts. He doesn't ask, "Do all prophesy?" It may be that many people in that Corinthian church had that spiritual gift but they were not considered prophets. A person with a ministry is someone anointed by God, (that is with a recognized spiritual authority) to exercise a gift consistently and regularly as part of the work of building up the church. In the first part of verse 28, Paul establishes three ministries: apostles, prophets, and teachers. In Ephesians 4, evangelists and pastors are added to the list. All the other gifts are open to everyone as well as being employed by those in any of the five ministries. So healing – like working miracles, helping others, administration, speaking in tongues, interpretation, faith, wisdom, discernment – is a gift we may manifest from time to time, along with other gifts, for the edification of the church. Jesus confirms this when He commissioned His disciples after His resurrection:

> *Go into all the world and preach the good news to all creation. Whoever believes and is baptized will be saved, but whoever does not believe will be condemned. And these signs will accompany those who believe: In my name they will drive out demons, they will speak in new tongues; they will pick up snakes with their hands; and when they drink deadly poison, it will not hurt them at all; they will place their hands on sick people, and they will get well.*

So anyone who believes may exercise miraculous gifts, but in reality, as Paul observes, not everyone does believe. There are certain people who definitely should, and they are those with the five-fold ministry. Healings and miracles, we read in Scripture, accompany people whom God had called to these roles. It seems then, that there are two ways of praying for the sick:

1. Out of our faith ("those who believe");
2. Out of our God-appointed position of responsibility in the church.

What a difference it would make if people in these offices realized that God has promised that healing will be a natural extension of their ministry. Instead of wondering whether they have enough faith to pray for someone to be healed, they would know they have authority to do so. God has appointed and empowered them to manifest this gift in the course of fulfilling their particular role of leadership.

So in a sense, a healing ministry, in isolation from any other spiritual office, doesn't really exist. Those who are called "healers" are either people who have a strong degree of faith in the God who heals and are able frequently to bring His gifts of healing to sick people; or they are apostles, prophets teachers, pastors or evangelists who exercise the healing ministry as part of their responsibility towards the body of Christ and have been labelled "healers" by people whose eyes are caught more by this spectacular element in their ministry than any other.

God has increased my faith in His ability to use me as a channel of His healing, and there have been many instances when He has actually given me a gift of faith which has enabled me to bring His healing in situations which would normally be way beyond my everyday, personal faith. But basically, I have been called to preach the gospel and to teach, and people get healed in my meetings partly as a by-product of receiving that ministry. It is the anointing on my spiritual office that gives me the authority and power and confidence to pray for the sick.

Let us look more carefully, then, at who has gifts of healings. And notice it is plural – gifts of healing(s) implying that healing is not a power that we possess, but a new gift of health given individually to the sick person. The gift is for the one who is ill, not the one who prays.

## Apostles

Paul considered that his main ministry was that of an apostle, though he was undoubtedly an evangelist and a teacher as well. In 2 Corinthians 12:12, we read:

*The things that mark an apostle – signs, wonders and miracles – were done among you with great perseverance.*

We know from his own testimony, and from Luke's record in Acts, that one of the miraculous works Paul did was healing. Many of the men I have spoken to who are apostles have suggested that church-building is their sign: the charismatic groups and fellowships they have established are seen by them as the sign or wonder that validates their ministry. But I suggest the church building should be their fruit not their sign. Building churches is what they are supposed to do; but there is an added dimension of performing miracles to attest to their ministry. A true apostle should establish churches and bring in the kingdom, and Jesus said the kingdom of God was near when He healed the sick, cast out demons and worked miracles. So when an apostle seeks to establish a church in a community, he should proclaim the coming of the kingdom by healing the sick and working a few miraculous signs, preaching the word with signs following. By doing this, he establishes spiritual authority, the lordship of Christ mediated through his ministry, and the people will be much more likely to listen when he goes back to preach next time. His kingdom authority will draw out the other ministries and he will then be able to encourage these people in the exercise of their governmental gifts.

So to these apostolic brethren I say, "Next time you go to an area, offer to pray for the sick. Don't wait for a word of knowledge. Pray for them because you already have gifts of healing for them in your spiritual office." Some apostles have gone off and done this, and some mighty things have happened because they had the confidence that they have healing gifts to share as a result of their calling.

## Prophets

God has always wanted to make His will known to His people in order to draw men, women, nations, and peoples back to Himself for their benefit, blessing, and security. For this reason God raised up prophets who would lead His people out of their enemies' hands and into His purposes for their time and generation. The Old Testament prophets had an unusually difficult task persuading the people to believe their words and to believe in Jehovah as the only true God. They certainly suffered their share of rejection and had to maintain a clear line of communication from God. To show His reality and presence, God graciously attested to the prophets' word with powerful signs and wonders. The prophet was in one sense a sign pointing to an invisible God who wanted to make Himself to His people.

Elijah and Elisha called down fire from heaven, transformed poisonous food and water, provided for the widow in time of famine, fed one hundred people on twenty loaves with food to spare, cleansed the leper, raised the dead, and more. They brought the power of God to bear in every type of situation whether in the material, physical, or spiritual realms.

When Jesus came along and declared He was a prophet it was because of the miracles that He performed. The signs of a prophet were upon His life so that when Jesus raised the widow's son from the dead everyone was "filled with great awe and praised God."

> …"A great prophet has appeared among us," they said. "God has come to help his people" (Luke 7:16).

Jesus as the prophet and King spoke the word and it came to pass: water was turned to wine, the hungry were fed, the demonized were set free, and the dead were raised, showing that the Kingdom of God had come. The words of the prophet are truly in deed and power and the same signs should accompany a prophet's ministry as he proclaims the will of the Lord.

### Evangelists and Teachers

An evangelist preaches to the unsaved and proclaims the good news of salvation through Jesus' death and resurrection. A teacher preaches to the saved, being able to communicate revelation truth from the Word of God in a simple manner. What they have in common is that they both preach the Word which God promises to confirm with signs and wonders. In the Early Church, one man often fulfilled the two functions since new converts had no other source of teaching.

Again and again in the New Testament, we see the miraculous (and that undoubtedly included healing) accompanying preaching of the Word. Paul, in fact, seemed to think it was the essence of proclaiming the Gospel of Christ:

> I will not venture to speak of anything except what Christ has accomplished through me in leading the Gentiles to obey God by what I have said and done – by the power of signs and miracles, through the power of the Spirit. So from Jerusalem all the way around to Illyricum, I have fully proclaimed the gospel of Christ (Romans 15:18-19).

Again in Hebrews, he inextricably links signs and wonders preaching of the Gospel:

> *We must pay more careful attention, therefore, to what we have heard, so that we do not drift away…This salvation, which was first announced by the Lord, was confirmed to us by those who heard him. God also testified to it by signs, wonders and various miracles, and gifts of the Holy Spirit distributed according to his will* (Hebrews 2:1, 3, 4).

Look at the evangelist Philip when he went down to Samaria. He didn't preach healing, he preached Christ. And when you preach Christ, you get healings.

> *Those who had been scattered preached the word wherever they went. Philip went down to a city in Samaria and proclaimed Christ there. When the crowds heard Philip and saw the miraculous signs he did, they all paid close attention to what he said. With shrieks, evil spirits came out of many, and many paralytics and cripples were healed. So there was great joy in that city*
> (Acts 8:4-8 [emphasis added]).

Perhaps, particularly an evangelist should think of himself as a travelling salesman (for that company he works for: Father, Son, and Holy Ghost Unlimited). No self-respecting salesman would go around without free samples; he would never sell anything. And God has an unlimited supply of free samples. Freely you have received, freely give.

I recently heard about an evangelist who preached in India to crowds of a hundred and fifty thousand, and after preaching powerfully for two hours he invited people to give their lives to Christ. No one responded.

"Right," he said, "now I am going to demonstrate the Gospel to you."

He walked towards the crowd and selected three individuals who were in need of physical healing. There was a blind man, a woman born deaf and dumb, and finally a woman so crippled and deformed that she could only move on the palms of her hands and the heels of her feet.

He returned to the platform with these sick people and a quietness descended on the crowd. He rebuked Satan as he prayed for the blind man and instantly the man could see. The evangelist then commanded Satan to let loose the deaf and dumb woman, and proceeded to heal her by teaching her to speak in English. Finally, he turned to the crowd and said, "I have not come here to fight against your god. Let us all pray to Allah that this woman who is still badly crippled will be healed." After a time of joint prayer he noted to the crowd that the woman was still sick and informed them that it was because their god was dead. He then shouted in a loud voice, "Satan, loose your hold over this woman." Immediately the power of God came over her body, and she stood upright on her feet. After seeing that, the crowd erupted and many thousands decided that night to forsake their god and serve the Lord Jesus Christ.

This is true evangelism on a large scale using the gifts of the Holy Spirit, for as God's Word has stated, "He will confirm the word with signs following" (Mark 16:15-18).

The evangelist knew that because of his office in the church he had access to gifts of healings for the people as he boldly proclaimed the Gospel. His faith was in the authority that God had placed within him as a holder of one of the fivefold ministries in the church of Jesus Christ. He knew that he represented the Kingdom of God, and just as a commercial traveller would carry samples of his company, the evangelist knew that he could rely totally upon God to give samples of the Kingdom.

## Pastors

I've heard some pastors say, "I'm just the shepherd of this church. You can't expect me to do the healing, too. I'm not the type."
But look at Ezekiel 34:

> ...*This is what the Sovereign Lord says, Woe to the shepherds of Israel who only take care of themselves. Should not shepherds take care of the flock? You eat the curds, clothe yourselves with the wool, and slaughter the choice animals, but you do not take care of the flock. You have not strengthened the weak or healed the sick or bound up the injured*... (Ezekiel 34:2-4).

And in Zechariah 10:2 we read,

> *The idols speak deceit,*
> *diviners see visions that lie;*
> *they tell dreams that are false,*
> *they give comfort in vain.*
> *Therefore the people wander like sheep oppressed for lack of a shepherd.*

Jesus said that a good shepherd looks after his sheep and knows them by name. His concern for them is such that should one of his flocks go missing he will leave the flock secure in the pen and go searching for the lost one until he finds it. He will carry it home if necessary, rub oil in the wounds

142

and care for it. He is a true shepherd and he would do the same for all of his sheep. If they are sick he seeks to see that they recover. They are valuable to him, and he does not leave them to fend for themselves.

In the same way God wants and expects His shepherds or pastors to love their people, to care for and to heal the sick ones amongst their flocks. God has shepherds or pastors in a high category in His list of offices in Ephesians 4:11. Within this ministry God has placed healing gifts to release the sick under that person's care, and it is the pastor's God-given privilege and responsibility to look after the people in this way.

In God's economy then, you don't generally take sheep to a vet, that is, a professional healer; you take them to the shepherd. So pastors have healing gifts for their sheep. Not for all sheep, just their own flock. This is why church membership is not optional but essential. We need to know where we are planted so that if we get sick we can go to our pastor and ask for prayer with both of us having confidence that he has the healing gift for us.

## Elders

> *Is any one of you sick? He should call the elders of the church to pray over him and anoint him with oil in the name of the Lord. And the prayer offered in faith will make the sick person well; the Lord will raise him up…* (James 5:14-16).

You are lying sick in your bed feeling dreadful and you feel you have to call the elders to pray for you. But looking up at their helpless faces you feel a whole lot worse, and listening to their conversation gives you complete confidence their prayer won't work: "Brother, do you feel led to pray? No, brother, you go ahead," and so on. They are worried about who has the faith, or who has the gift, instead of realizing that, as elders, they possess **corporately** the ability to heal the sick. God has implanted in their office the anointing to pray for the people under their oversight. God is very fair and if He calls you to a position of responsibility within the body, He will give you the ability to fulfil it. The anointing goes with the calling. So if you are an elder and you consistently have no ability, then it is possible you are not an elder in the Holy Ghost, that you are man-appointed, not God anointed. Many elders have no expectation of healing, and many church members do not have faith that their elders can pray for the sick because they know the men and all their failings. This puts pressure on both parties. However an eldership can and should draw strength and courage from God who has called them, who has promised them that they shall successfully pray for the sick because of their office in the church.

So if you get ill, call the elders of the church. Not just your favourite elder; all of them. Not the one you agree with, all of them. And they should all pray with the knowledge that in their office lies the authority to carry the gift of healing from God's hand into your body. There should be no tension, no fear, no striving. I've been prayed for once or twice when I have been ill, not in my home church, I hasten to add, and the fact that I didn't end up with a dislocated neck or a damaged spine has been purely by the grace of God, because I've not simply had hands laid on me, I've had people exerting all their strength in an endeavour to bring healing. They have never thought about being gentle, but have pressed and prayed fervently, and pressed a bit harder. You start with a headache and finish with concussion. In fact, I've seen some shake and push so much that the poor sick person got a headache just from the rings bouncing up and down on his head.

James goes on to say in the passage about elders praying for the sick:

> If he has sinned, he will be forgiven. Therefore confess your sins to each other, and pray for each other so that you may be healed.

So the elders should ask, "Have you got any confessions to make?" And sometimes the sick person replies, "Yes, I don't believe you should be an elder, and I'm afraid I can't stand you."

Now that situation is a non-starter. For healing to take place in this context, the sick person must respect the authority of the eldership, and the elders must be confident of the calling and anointing. Unless there is loving submission and loving authority, there will be no channel for the Holy Spirit to flow through as we have already seen the blockages caused by resentment and an unsubmissive heart. So there must be repentance and reconciliation.

> A heart at peace gives life to the body, but envy [or resentment, rebellion, criticism] rots the bones (Proverbs 14:30).

Notice that this passage says that if you are sick, you call the elders. The onus is on the sick person. Don't expect the elders to go around visiting with a pot of oil for anointing, and discovering by chance the people who need prayer. Get on the telephone and ask them to come to see you.

**House Group Leaders**

Like pastors and elders, house group leaders have gifts of healing for the small flock under their care. They have assumed spiritual authority over the

144

people in their group and should have confidence to pray for them when they get ill.

Some years ago I went to a church which was keen on structure and authority and had just split up into house groups. I was interested to see whether all this structure was building a house or just a piece of scaffolding, so in the meeting I picked on one brother and asked him how many he had in his house group.

"Ten," he answered.

"How many are sick?"

"All ten."

"Wonderful," I said, "bring them all forward."

So they all stood up and I asked them who was the sickest among them. One man, about six-foot-three stood up and said, "I've got ulcerative colitis."

"That's fine," I replied, "we'll start with the worst and work down."

And turning to the house group leader, I asked, "Have you prayed for him?"

The poor man was nearly crying. I'm sure he was wishing I had never been invited, but he stuck with it and said, "Yes, I've prayed. I've prayed, sought God, been on a three week fast…"

My, what love, I thought. I've never fasted for anyone's healing for three weeks.

"…but nothing happens."

"You've prayed in faith," I explained gently, "and the problem is that in your heart you do not believe God is going to do it through you. Would you pray for this brother again, please?"

"But I've prayed for him three or four times," the leader cried desperately.

"That's OK," I said, "just come out here, put your hand up to heaven and receive the gift of healing."

He obviously thought I was strange, to say the least! This man was well educated, he had attended university, had a top-grade job, and now he was being asked to do something completely irrational.

"What on earth do you mean?" he asked, bewildered.

"Faith is the substance of something you hope for. Do you hope for this brother to be healed?"

"Oh yes, I really do," he replied earnestly.

"It is the evidence of something not seen. The evidence is in your imagination. So if he needs a new colon, just imagine receiving it from head office. God's got a warehouse in heaven with all the spare parts we need. He will send a new colon by express delivery to your hand, if you just put up your hand like a little child and receive it."

"But how will I know I've got it?" he asked worriedly.

"Because with the eyes of your spirit you will see it."

After a few minutes the leader said, "I can see a piece of straw, or maybe it's a piece of tubing."

"Now put your hand on this man's head and pray for him in the name of Jesus." I said.

So he put his hand lightly on the tall man's head and prayed. The recipient of the prayer went down under the power of God; I thought he would damage his back, but not only was that all right but all his pain had gone.

The house group leader stood staring at his hand, saying, "I don't believe it! I don't believe it!"

"Well, you don't need me," I told him, "I'm just going to have a cup of coffee and I'll be back in a few minutes." Fifteen minutes later, there were nine more people lying on the floor healed, his entire house group! He certainly was not praying out of his faith. He was praying out of his office, his position of responsibility in the body of Christ.

The next night we had a meeting in the town hall and over eight hundred people came. This leader was so excited by all that had happened that he said

146

to me, "Brother, I feel I could pray tonight."

So I said fine, called a healing line, and told him to carry on. We prayed for many people that night and two hundred or so were healed. He prayed for twenty-five and according to him, none of them were healed. Driving home together afterwards, he was crying.

"You see," he said bitterly. "It's just your faith that makes things work. When you're not there, nothing happens."

So I asked the Lord why it didn't work, and He replied, "They weren't his sheep. He had authority for his ten, but not over hundreds or thousands or ten thousands. He stepped outside his anointing."

This is a wonderful truth to enable people to pray from an authority position but it must always be held in tension with the fact that Jesus said to all His disciples: "If you can believe, all things are possible, to him who believes."

## Parents

When praying for your child, it is so easy to let your own emotions take control, "Oh Lord, you know how much I love little Johnny…"

And God says, "Yes, and I love him far more than you do…"

When we try and plead with God on the basis of how much our child means to us, we get caught up with fear and tension. Pray for your children as priests, not as parents. Stand before God and pray for your family with authority, bringing the healing gifts for your children which God has anointed you.

This will work almost 100 percent of the time when your children are very small because they haven't learned to doubt. But by the time they are six or seven, you may be getting problems. The children will have discovered television and will see people taking yellow pills and blue pills, and red medicine, and it's not long before they want to try these things. Then when they get to school, everyone is getting inoculated and injected, and they want it too. By this time, they will have to use their own faith. But initially they can be healed on your faith as you stand as the representative before God, and minister His life to them. Before you pray for your child, go to God and receive their healing in the spirit, because empty hands laid on empty heads are no good for anyone!

And how do you know you have the gift? You can see it. Spiritual perception, I call it, rather than simply imagination, you can see with the eyes of your spirit, the vague outline of the body part that you need.

Do you realize that there are almost no prayers for healing in the New Testament? Instead, authority is taken over the disease. And God delegates kingdom authority to us. The Roman centurion whose servant was sick said to Jesus,

> *"Lord, don't trouble yourself, for I do not deserve to have you come under my roof. That is why I did not even consider myself worthy to come to you. But say the word, and my servant will be healed. For I myself am a man under authority, with soldiers under me. I tell this one, 'Go,' and he goes; and that one, 'Come,' and he comes. I say to my servant, 'Do this,' and he does it"* (Luke 7:7-8).

You too, Jesus, are a man under authority, he is saying. And Jesus conferred that same authority on those who believed and followed Him. A pastor, for example, is like a spiritual policeman. If you see a policeman standing in the middle of the road with his hand up, you will do your best to stop because he is on duty and has his uniform on. If you hit him, all the police force in the country will be after you. Now he doesn't have the physical strength in his hand to stop you and your thirty-two ton truck, but he's not standing in his own strength but in the authority of the law.

# Praying from God's Perspective

Jesus never prayed from earth to heaven. He was a citizen of heaven who prayed down to earth. He never struggled to get out from beneath problems; He looked down on them and told them to be cast into the sea.

> *And God raised us up with Christ and seated us with him in the heavenly realms in Christ Jesus* (Ephesians 2:6).

We can see and deal with sickness from God's perspective, and there are five steps to do this:

## 1. Think God's Thoughts

Don't think, "What are we going to do with this poor person?" Think what God thinks: "I'm going to heal him, hallelujah." You look down on the problem and think in the name of Jesus, that he is going to be healed.

## 2. Feel God's Emotions When You Pray

So many people pray with a tremendous burden, with great fervour and intensity which is really a cover up for unbelief. When you pray for someone in the hospital and you are discouraged by the sight of how ill they are, then turn your back on them and look at Jesus. Start praying and praising the Lord and you will feel joy, because in His presence there is fullness of joy. You can declare with confidence, "I've come to bring the kingdom of God to you, hallelujah!"

## 3. Understand God's Plan

Know that you are not praying simply because the person is sick, you are praying to extend the reign of Christ's righteousness because of His government, there shall be no end. Seek first the kingdom of God, and all these things shall be added to you. When you pray, ask for God's will to be done on earth as it is in heaven. Is there sickness in heaven? No. Is there cancer in heaven? No. So Christ's reign on earth means health and wholeness. You shouldn't need a rhema word to tell you that; a basic knowledge of God's character should be enough. Once we pray from a kingdom viewpoint, we have the right perspective.

## 4. Pray What God Tells You to Pray

There is much confusion and argument in the church if a Christian can have a demon, or a demon have a Christian. I do not believe that an evil spirit can possess a Christian. But I do think that a great deal of sickness, perhaps 60 percent, is initiated by an evil spirit, and as Christians, we can be oppressed, bound, vexed, and depressed by them.

If you trip and fall headlong down a flight of stairs, you are unlikely (unless you are my wife) to bounce down saying, "Praise the Lord, Hallelujah, thank you, Jesus, Amen." Most of us scream. And when we react in panic and fear, we are in the devil's realm. In that moment of terror, it is possible for him to place a spirit of infirmity into our spinal column, which may prevent our back from fully recovering after treatment, which may cause the whole area to be weak afterwards. Now, if we simply pray for healing the physical damage, this is what may happen: as the healing power of God floods into our body, the spirit of infirmity goes further down and hides because it doesn't like the sudden influx of the Holy Spirit. But after three or four days, it comes up again and when it expresses itself it will be painful, often worse than before.

Here are a few illustrations from real life. I prayed for an elder once and the situation might have been amusing if it had not been so distressing for him. He had terrible sinus problems, so I said to him, "That's no problem. I will get the pastor of your church to come and pray for you, and you will be healed." So the pastor laid hands on him and commanded him to be healed in the name of Jesus. At once he could breathe properly through his nose and everything was marvellous, until three days later when I received a telephone call from him:

"Three days ago, I just had sinus trouble," he said, "now I have bronchial asthma."

I am afraid I almost laughed. But at least it had shown me that a spirit, which had taken cover when we prayed and was now reacting with a vengeance, had caused his sinus trouble. I took authority over his asthma and cast it out. He was never troubled by it from that day. Now I knew I was addressing a spiritual force or being, but I didn't say, "Come out, you spirit of asthma," because that would have probably caused him more fear and confusion. However, a spirit was cast out without any violent reactions. I believe that if you are moving in the authority, there need not necessarily be dramatic manifestations of evil. Let us briefly look at how Jesus dealt with the problem:

*When evening came, many who were demon-possessed were brought to him, and he drove out the spirits with a word and healed the sick. This was to fulfil what was spoken through the prophet Isaiah, "He took up our infirmities and carried our diseases"* (Matthew 8:16-17).

When Jesus cast out spirits, healing took place. The devil was not allowed to get attention. And He cast them out **with a word**, not with repeated shouting or rebuking. If I come against a spirit of infirmity in someone's back, I look for a manifestation of freedom. He or she should scream with joy, not fear, as the disc slips back into place. Sometimes unpleasant manifestations can't be helped, but generally I don't think they edify.

If a person has to go into the hospital for a general anaesthetic, it is wise to surround them in prayer, because I have seen people who go into the hospital for relatively easy operations who have come out with postoperative depression. On occasions, I have come against the spirit of infirmity and the person has returned to normal.

Many people who experience traumatic road accidents, who are thrown through the windshield, land on their head in the highway, and suffer epileptic fits afterwards. Now some epilepsy, I am convinced is a sickness caused by certain forms of illnesses such as meningitis. But in other cases, it is caused by trauma, and when we pray for someone in this instance, we should take authority over a spirit.

We need to recognize that just because we have the gift of healing for someone, they will not necessarily be healed instantaneously by the laying-on of hands. We need wisdom to know how to deal with each problem. Jesus prayed for one man who was deaf by casting out a spirit. On another occasion, He touched a man's ear and healed him.

A woman came to me some years ago with a terrible pain. She did not know what it was so I asked the Lord what was causing it. It was a fear of cancer. And when I questioned her, I found that Uncle George had died of cancer. Aunt Sally had died of cancer, it was in her family and eventually it would get her. As soon as she had the slightest pain she imagined it was cancer, and the tension and fear aggravated the pain. A spirit had got into her body, lying to her, wearing her down, so that her life was dominated by this fear. When the root of fear was dealt with the physical problem was healed.

## 5. Trust God with the Supernatural

When you have done what you can, you must fall back on the faithfulness of God to do what only He can do. He promises He will confirm the word with signs following. Striving and fretting will only block the flow of His power.

On a practical level, when ministering to individuals, make certain that they give you their full attention. If they have understood your explanation of the Bible verses about healing, (and question them to ascertain whether or not this is so) tell them what you are going to do next: that you are going to command the pain to leave them in Jesus' name, or that you are about to lay hands upon them and to ask for the presence of the Holy Spirit to come over them. If you, as the minister, sense an outpouring of love, or joy, or deep peace, communicate this as well, as all these steps help release faith and enable the person being prayed over to receive from God. Pray from heavenly places down into their need, or bring God's will in heaven into their piece of earth.

There must be cooperation between the person praying and the one who is trying to receive from God. When this is achieved, the Holy Spirit gains a channel through which He can operate. When casting out a spirit of grief, trust God to bring the release of joy, or if it is depression, look for the peace of God to flood into the person. We cannot produce these emotions or psych them up, but we can and must stand in a position of faith until we can see that God has brought the manifestation of healing. We must remember that we are not dealing with natural problems but fighting a war against spiritual problems with outward manifestations. We have authority over the evil forces belonging to the devil.

Many people in the Bible were healed "in the same hour," or as they went upon their way, acting upon the words of Jesus. We are sometimes called upon to believe God in spite of our lingering symptoms.

In our capacity as healing ministers, we can break through this interim problem by holding the answer in our faith until the person can receive healing for himself or herself. We can always tell whether we have prayed in faith because of the joy level that becomes present inside us:

> *Until now you have not asked for anything in my name. Ask and you will receive, and your joy will be complete* (John 16:24).

So we must stand in the gap between man and God and **He will do** the miraculous.

# How to Organize a Healing Service

A healing service requires proper organization. The leader, organizer, worship leader, and speaker will all possibly be subjected to spiritual attack  and certain precautions must be  taken and  certain  practical considerations need to be heeded.

## BEFORE YOU BEGIN

### Be Completely Dependent on God

We must cultivate a total dependence on God when praying for the sick, realizing from the outset that no matter how much knowledge, experience, or how many times we have prayed for the sick, we cannot use the Holy Spirit. He refuses to be used; He uses us. We must put our faith in the God who heals and be totally convinced that it is His will to deliver people from sickness.

### Be Led by the Spirit, Not Pressed by Personalities

It is important in a ministry not to feel under pressure to visit a certain group just because you are free and you feel that you cannot refuse the invitation. This problem is particularly common when starting out and you may be tempted to go where God has not gone before you. This has happened many times in our lives. A need does not constitute a calling. It is important to establish what both you and the group require before you accept an invitation. Ask questions. See that you really are the ministry they need at that time. Is your ministry going to fit in with their overall strategy? What is the reason for holding the meeting? Where are the people in their walk with God? How many people do they expect to attend? Would it be better to teach a faith clinic in an afternoon session and then hold an evening outreach service? What about financial commitment? It is better to be open and talk things through before plunging blindly into a situation. You will end up appreciating each other far more.

# MAKING YOUR PLANS

## Choose the Right Building

Much depends on the size of a fellowship and their maturity to determine the size of the hall that should be rented. Healing meetings depend on atmosphere, and it will be a big mistake to get over enthusiastic and rent an enormous hall, only to have it one quarter full with people.

If the sponsoring group is small, it will be out of proportion to expect a thousand people to attend the meeting. So why go to all the trouble of setting out all the chairs "in faith"? It is far better to have a hall half the size and fill it. There is far more sense of excitement and anticipation when it is difficult to find a seat. When Kathryn Kuhlman had her meetings in Pittsburgh, PA, the large church building always seemed too small. She liked it that way, so that people exercised faith to attend the services. Many travelled hundreds of miles to attend and arrived hours early just to be certain of getting a seat in the meeting. It was not uncommon to hear of people being healed on the journey to the meeting or as they stood for hours in line waiting for the auditorium to open.

Always rent the building longer than you estimate you will need it! The Holy Spirit will not be rushed and time is needed for Him to move and to build up faith to a point where the deeper needs of people can be met. There are realms and depths of the Holy Spirit that we do not generally touch due to lack of time allocated to an evening service. The time has come where it is necessary to hold meetings lasting four or five hours for healing and salvation, where the crowds can come and get their needs met and experience the power of God.

First impressions are often lasting, therefore the choice of venue is important. A cold, badly-lit hall is not very welcoming or practical. Is the building easily accessible to people who suffer from disabilities? Is there an adequate parking facility for cars and buses? Are all questions that need answers addressed? Fire requirements and safety issues also need to be investigated.

## Lighting

Good lighting is very important. We have had some strange experiences that took place in rural areas, where it might prove difficult to rent a public building for the meeting. On one occasion we discovered that the spotlights in the hall were red, green and blue and shone directly onto the platform; reading the Bible was impossible! We tried to turn them off and we were left with just one blinding spotlight. As we peered in the general direction of the congregation, all we could see were spots in front of our eyes. Eye contact with the audience is essential, especially when giving out words of knowledge and looking to see who is responding.

## Use Wisdom in Stewarding

When holding a healing meeting, it is essential to realize that you will attract people from all backgrounds, and that they will be attending with various motivations. Some, who genuinely love the Lord, will be there to support the meeting. Others will be present because other Christians have invited them, or because they saw the advertisement in the newspaper. Some will be in faith, others in fear, scepticism, or tension. Therefore, it is important to have stewards welcome the congregation, show them to their seats and make quite certain that anyone acting strangely is prevented from sitting in any prominent position near the front. It is also recommended that any really serious cases be placed to one side away from the general congregation's attention.

## Do Not Isolate the Speaker

Ideally the platform should have sufficient room to accommodate the entire supporting local team and worship group. Faith can be created for the speaker to launch off if there is a sense of teamwork on the platform. The speaker is not a floating arm unattached to the body. He needs to be identified with the local vision and flow with the leadership of the meeting. A further recommendation would be that a robust lectern or stand be provided, with sufficient light for the minister to read the Bible.

## BEFORE THE SERVICE

### Enter into Spiritual Warfare

If you follow these suggestions, you will have the blueprint for the meeting in your grasp before you start. On several occasions I have spent time binding and loosing. If I ask the Lord what spiritual powers are influencing the meetings, He might show me a spirit of rebellion, and I would bind that and let loose the spirit of salvation. In other words, I bind the enemy and loosen the opposite work of the Holy Spirit.

Sometime ago the Lord led me to do this in a church in Chicago. The elders and I met together before the meeting, and as it is in many American churches, it was all very organized and businesslike. A woman sat in the corner taking shorthand to keep a record of the prayers, while the rest of us prayed, binding and loosing as the Lord directed. That evening over 90 percent of what had been prayed for earlier was healed without the slightest effort. It was as if all the unbelief and rebellion had been broken down, and the whole meeting was surrounded in God's glory.


## LEADING THE MEETING

### Enter into His Gates with Thanksgiving and His Courts with Praise

Always commence every meeting with prayer, welcome the Holy Spirit into the midst and ask God's blessing on the gathering. This prayer time will release people from their natural tension from attending a healing service and cause them to feel part of the program rather than visitors.

We need to be very sensitively led by the Spirit in this area of praise and worship when we hold healing meetings. For praise is the runway by which we ascend into the heavens and worship, and it is in this position of openness to God that people are most frequently and easily healed. So stay in the realm of praise until the majority of the congregation is drawn into the presence of God, and then progress into worshipful songs. Do not try to go at the commencement of the meeting, into a realm of worship, as many non-believers will not understand what is happening.

Ask how many people are in such a meeting for the first time. If you are holding a series of meetings, it is helpful to ask how many people have been significantly healed. You can then ask some of them to come forward and testify what God has done for them. That will build faith in others and deal with any scepticism.

Some pastors prefer to leave any offering to the end of the service to obtain a larger amount for the speaker. In my opinion, the best place in a service to take up the offering is after the praise section and before entering into worship. At the end of the service many people are involved in either praying or being prayed for and do not wish to be distracted from the presence of God to take up an offering.

If there is a special soloist, introduce him or her after the offering has been taken up, and before worship to ensure active participation of the congregation. It is best to put on the soloist before the speaker commences his message. But do not put the soloist on immediately prior to the speaker, as the congregation will be in passive mode and will find it more difficult to rise in their faith level.

Once the level of anointing has risen and people begin to worship, do not mix songs between praise and worship. Allow the worship hymns to build up to even higher levels.

Finally, at the end of the service, encourage people to stay and pray or worship; meanwhile, keep the musicians playing worshipful songs in the background. This helps to maintain the Lord's presence and facilitate the prayers of the ministry teams.

If you utilize ministry teams, have them wear badges that clearly distinguish them from the rest of the congregation, and either have them work as teams of two, or regulate the numbers that are qualified and trusted to pray for members of the opposite sex. Set these individuals apart by having them wear a different identifying badge. Have ushers walk around to ensure only people with badges are praying. Encourage ministry team members to attend sessions for personal prayer prior to the official start of the meeting.

## PREACHING THE MESSAGE

Pray before you start speaking. It not only draws the congregation together, but allows you to be God-conscious. It also helps calm stage fright when you are just starting out.

Include some humour in your message to relax the congregation so that it is easier for them to receive the Word of God.

Always include personal testimony and testimonies from others who have been healed. This always builds faith in the ears of the listeners and will help to facilitate their own healing later.

For the beginner in ministry, have an outline of what you want to say, but do not say everything you know. A short punchy message delivered in faith will do more than an exhaustive exposition of healing in the Scripture.

Be sensitive to the movement of the Holy Spirit. There will be times when, as you speak, the Holy Spirit's presence will supernaturally descend upon the meeting. When this happens, find a place where you can break off from the message and give the Holy Spirit freedom to do His works.

## THE TIME OF HEALING MINISTRY

As you preach, illustrations of healings will come to your mind. When this happens, treat them as possible "words of knowledge," and unless God indicates otherwise, coincide the healing time by calling out people with those very illnesses. This will undoubtedly build faith when they are healed. If God has used you in a particular healing before, then you know that He wants to always heal that problem through your ministry. So be confident when you pray, tell the person receiving prayer that God has already done this before and that will help to build them up as well.

If there seems to be a delay in information coming through from the Holy Spirit, it may be that there are other people present who have the same complaint as the person who has just received healing. Do not panic; ask if anyone else is suffering from the affliction. Remember it is God's perfect will to heal ALL!

Sometimes a person will come for prayer with a multitude of problems.

Isolate one illness that you can pray for in confidence, and pray for that specific problem; tell the person that is what you will do. When the particular malady is healed, it will release faith in the person to receive for his other problems.

Always, always, always have someone by your side that is skilled in catching people as they fall under the power of the Holy Spirit; never pray for anyone without a catcher being present. Since we live in a litigious society, it is essential that safety measures be always in place.

Occasionally, there will be someone in the healing line that has misunderstood how to receive from God. That person may start to praise or pray, possibly in tongues, during your prayer, believing erroneously that this will help the healing process. Politely ask them to stop praying, and to relax. This will unwittingly place the person in a posture to receive as God now has a receptive channel into which He can pour His healing power.

Maintain control over the meeting. You may call out a "word of knowledge" and have someone in the meeting try to suggest that it might be something different but similar. Be polite but firm and reiterate your word; they will come forward, if you stand your ground.

Be aware that people will react differently to the presence of the Holy Spirit. Remember that the Holy Spirit always directs the attention to the Lord Jesus. If someone is reacting violently to the ministration of the Spirit and is drawing attention, have an usher quietly lead him or her off to a private area to prevent distracting anyone else.

When the meeting is over and you feel drained of energy, seek prayer from the team to fill you up again! You have poured out life for several hours and you need a refilling.

Finally, after the service, if you cannot sleep and the meeting is being repeated over and over in your mind, it can be an indication that you are "holding" the Glory in some way. Pray and thank God for the healings, His presence, using you and then offer Him back the Glory. You will then fall asleep!

## TWO THINGS LEADERS NEED TO DO

I believe that God is going to start putting apostolic teams of healing ministries together. It will be essential to recognize that we are not in competition. There will be brothers and sisters who are consistently used by God in certain realms of miracles, and we need to be able to recognize the different gifts to the Body of Christ without feeling inadequate or rejected. We must stand together, if we are going to learn from the failures of the past.

By way of example, when people come after a meeting requesting prayer, I normally refer them to my wife, Rosemary. She is more compassionate and is more equipped to spend time with them in counselling before prayer; therefore, they will be more likely to get their needs met through her ministry. If I was sharing a platform with Dr. James Maloney and someone came with a skeletal deformity, I would prefer that he prayed. This is not lack of faith on my part but, as God uses him especially in this area, I would seek to honour him and recognize God's vessel.

As leaders, we need to become familiar with the working of the "gifts of the Holy Spirit" and to make use of them regularly. Basically, there are three gifts we control: prophecy, tongues, and interpretation of tongues; and six which are in the control of the Holy Spirit: the word of knowledge, the word of wisdom, the gifts of healing, the working of miracles, the discerning of spirits, and gifts of faith. This is a sensitive issue because in the Bible we find no teaching on how the power gifts work and so they are open to abuse, or attempts at abuse. But they are supposed to flow out of a life of worship and consecration to God, it means dedicating ourselves to God's service. He can use us if we are yielded to the Holy Spirit, relaxed and waiting for Him to move.

One aspect of moving out in the gifts is that every time we step out, when we are commencing in ministry, a great trench of fear us challenges us. But as we worship God and go beyond our fears, our earthen vessels become filled with the treasures of God.

It is important to include briefly, how to recognize the "word of knowledge" because this is, undoubtedly, a very powerful tool in the armoury of the minister. This gift usually manifests itself in five ways: you may hear a voice, you may see a picture in your spirit, you may simply have a sense of knowing, you may feel pain or other sensation in your body, or you may receive an open vision. The point to remember is that the information only comes once, and at the beginning, it is always followed by doubts!

# The Healing Ministry: A Price to Pay

God has been leading us more and more to teach others how to pray for the sick. It is for this reason that we have been holding training seminars throughout the world. Judging by the response, it seems people are really keen to become involved. So many people have benefited already and we have had very encouraging reports from those who have stepped into a healing ministry and started to pray for the sick.

In view of this enthusiasm, I feel it is very important to point out that there is considerable cost involved and it is an area where we can be very vulnerable. Having been engaged full-time in this ministry for over thirty years, I have had my fair share of experiences, some of which I would not like to repeat; but I can at least pass on to you what the Lord has shown me through them. It is easy to look back and laugh when the actual experience is way behind you, but at the time it can be extremely painful. You suffer, you make your nearest and dearest suffer with you, and often, someone else has to pick up the pieces.

Many people are obviously attracted by the thought of being able to perform miracles. But if that is our motivation, whether unconsciously or altruistically (I will be able to help so many people), then we probably won't see any. For more than any other ministry – because in reality no one can produce the miraculous through his own ability or strength-healing requires a complete surrender of our own life. A person can appear to be an inspired preacher but in fact he is simply is an eloquent speaker who can deliver a brilliant sermon (intellectually) without needing the Spirit at all. No one can make a crippled person walk, or a person with terminal cancer live, unless the Holy Spirit within touches the person who is sick. It is from a position of complete weakness and surrender that God leads us into a ministry of healing. We are thoroughly dependent on His Spirit.

It takes a long time to realize the truth of Jesus' words:

> *Except a corn of wheat fall onto the ground and die, it abides alone, but if it dies it brings forth much fruit.*

We know that Jesus has already died in our place, but we have to identify with it to bring forth fruit out of that death. Paul exhorts the believers in Rome:

> *Therefore, I urge you, brothers, in view of God's mercy, to offer your bodies as living sacrifices, holy and pleasing to God, this is your spiritual act of worship*
> (Romans 12:1 [emphasis added]).

Because of God's goodness to us, we have received what we don't deserve, that is, His redemption with all its benefits through His sacrifice for us, we should give our whole lives over to Him. This is a once and for all experience when we accept His salvation and Lordship of our lives, but it is also an ongoing commitment which is tested at various points in our lives as we move forward in faith. We may be like Peter who was very extroverted and was raring to go, or we may be like Moses who was afraid to speak, but in both instances their lives were refined and their commitment tested as they responded to God's call. It wasn't an easy life for them, and it won't necessarily be easy for us, but in all the trials of faith and seemingly depressing circumstances, Jesus is there to encourage us to rise up and walk on.

James is able to view his own difficulties and trials for being a follower of Christ in a remarkable light:

> *Consider it pure joy, my brothers, whenever you face trials of many kinds, because you know that the testing of your faith develops perseverance. Perseverance must finish its work so that you may be mature and complete, not lacking anything.* (James 1:2-4 [emphasis added]).

James obviously shared Jesus' vision of their joy that lay on the other side of the Cross. But I know "pure joy" isn't usually our reaction when problems arise especially when we have not walked this way before and every step is a new step of faith. It's easy to become discouraged or cynical, to blame our own failings, or God's people, or even God Himself. But God loves us too much for us to stay the way we are, and as we embark on ministry. He does a little pruning and character building here and there. As God said to a friend of ours once, "I am FOR you, not against you!"

Jesus wants us to know this, and by His encouragement and love He beckons us to walk on, to go deeper into the waters of His Spirit and swim in them (Ezekiel 47). In my own experience, I wanted to test the temperature of the water first – to put in my big toe and then my feet found their hold go a bit further amidst the stones and swift current. As we step out, we gradually find that our footing becomes less fearful and unsteady; once we get used to being knee deep, we dare to let go and plunge in until the water supports us completely. Entering the healing ministry is like going through the waters of baptism – it involves a kind of death as we allow our lives to be hidden in Christ.

Ironically, we will find that when we see miracles happen, when we pray for the sick, that this will make people criticize and reject us. "You can't do it that way," they say. "That's not scriptural," says another group. "It's all fixed," say the sceptics. Jesus said:

> *...The blind receive sight, the lame walk, those who have leprosy are cured, the deaf hear, the dead are raised, and the good news preached to the poor. Blessed is the man who does not fall away on account of me"* (Luke 7:22-23).

The Revised Standard Version says "Blessed is he who takes no offence at me." Even healing miracles won't win you a fan club; quite the opposite. People will often take offence and you will find you are being ostracized just when you thought you were getting established. You will be tempted to give up not only your ministry but your whole faith. But through all this, cling to the Lord. He rewards faithfulness and He promises to give the Spirit without measure to those who make Him Lord.

The Lord has His own training program and reward system. Sometimes He requires us to leave home and friends and to serve His purposes in some distant place. He then gives us His promise:

> *...No one who has left home or brothers or sisters or mother or father or children or fields for me and the gospel will fail to receive a hundred times as much in this present age (homes, brothers, sisters, mothers, children and fields – and with them, persecutions) and in the age to come, eternal life* (Mark 10:29-30).

We need to be dedicated in the face of apparent failure and in the face of success. Two people who had that tenacity, that vision, that boldness were Elijah and Elisha. First, look at Elijah in 1 Kings 19. One moment he was performing incredible miracles through the gift of faith on Mount Carmel, and the next he was sitting under a broom tree in the desert wishing he could die. Jezebel was out to murder him and he felt as if he had not a friend left in the world.

"I've had enough. Lord," he groaned, and exhausted with disillusion- ment and despair, he fell asleep. Be warned, this is a common situation after an intense outpouring of spiritual power. It happened to me once, when I was ministering in Sweden. The day started ordinarily. While I was praying before the afternoon service, I had a vision of an empty wheelchair. I was terrified. It was in the early days when I had absolutely no confidence anyone could be healed through my prayer, and I was sure I was going to be way out of my depth that evening. I tried desperately to think of how I could get out of going to the meeting. At four o'clock in the afternoon, I walked into the little church and there under the pulpit was this wretched wheelchair – occupied. I was feeling very afraid and so as I tried to preach faith, and the more I preached, the further into unbelief I got. Eventually, I thought I would do better to pray for the sick by the word of knowledge:

"Somebody here is suffering from a headache."

(That was about my level at that moment...) Someone responded and immediately the pain went.

"Somebody is suffering with sinus problems. You are now healed."

And a woman exclaimed, "Yes, it's me. It's wonderful!" After three or four successful words of knowledge, I suddenly felt a pressure across my chest and I said, "There's someone here who has difficulty in breathing."

And the dear old lady in the wheelchair squeaked. "It's me!"

For a moment I felt I could have made her gasp for her breath. But I rejected the thought quickly and went over to her.

"What's going to happen when I pray for you?" I asked.

"I'm going to stand up and walk," she replied without hesitation. "Yes, God has told me I'm going to be healed tonight."

There was no way out. I put my hand on her head and prayed, "Father, in the name of Jesus, heal her." Slump. She sank back into her wheelchair, but a second later she asked me to help her up. I was so frightened. I knew she wasn't healed and I was sure she would do herself terrible damage by trying to walk. But she insisted I helped her out of the wheelchair, and she staggered three or four steps before I saw an empty seat and thankfully guided her to it. Good, I thought, you can sit there and afterwards you can just go quietly home. But suddenly I sensed the presence of the Holy Spirit, and for the first time in my life I experienced the gift of faith. The anointing of God rained down upon me and I felt about six foot wide and nine foot tall. I did not have one doubt in my being. Then I heard the little old woman's voice saying "I have pain in my ankle."

It never occurred to me that she was sitting in the wheelchair because of her ankle. I thought she was there because she could not breathe properly. But looking down, I could see her grotesquely swollen ankle and as I took it in my hands, it felt just as if oil was flowing down through my hands and over her ankle. Instantly the swelling shrivelled before our eyes, and before I could stop her she had jumped up and was running around the church. When she came back I asked her what had been the matter with her leg and she explained that she had been sitting in the wheelchair for nineteen years, had received many operations on her foot and now had a steel bar going from the base of her foot up through her leg which meant she would never walk again.

I turned around and there was a man almost bent double leaning heavily on crutches. "Pray for me," he pleaded. I hardly knew what I was doing. I just stood under the anointing and said, "Be healed!" Suddenly my hand flew upwards as he straightened up like a soldier standing to attention, and the cancer of the hip disappeared as God put in place a new hip joint.

Next a lady with a huge goiter stood in front of me. It was hard to see her because her enlarged throat dominated her whole aspect. She tragically recounted that she had been an opera singer, but could no longer sing a note, since the hideous lump in her throat restricted it. Again, I could hardly believe the words which came out of my mouth, but I told her that I was going to touch the goiter and then she should start singing "Our Father, who art in Heaven." I placed my hand on the swelling and in a moment the church was filled with the most beautiful heavenly singing as she worshiped the Lord. The goiter vanished.

For the next ten days not a soul got healed, not one, not even from a cold. I came back from Sweden thinking, "Did that happen or not? Am I saved or am I not saved?" The intensity of that anointing had been so great, the feeling of confidence, energy, strength, and power so overwhelming, that when it lifted it was as if I plunged into the depths of despair. I hardly knew who or where I was. At times like that, it is a great help if you have someone in the family who is in the faith, like your wife, who doesn't go down with you but can encourage you. And it is also a great help if you have a strong and caring fellowship to support you.

Elijah was alone, of course. But in the absence of all human help, God sustained him and sent an angel to feed him and strengthen him so that he could carry on until he reached the place where God had planned to meet with him. In the loneliness of the cave, God invited him to pour out how he was really feeling. Out came all his hurt, rejection, indignation, and his sense of isolation. Yet he didn't curse God or put the blame on Him, though it would have been easy for him to be angry and wallow in self-pity.

He was still able to discern the voice of the Lord, a gentle whisper after all the drama and spectacle of the wind, the earthquake, and the fire as if he knew that despite the excitement of the miracles on Mount Carmel, his relationship with God and his ability to recognize the real presence of the Lord were paramount. He didn't hide from God with a sense of failure, guilt, and resentment but stood right before the Lord with total openness and honesty, and repeated his despair. He acknowledged that he had come to an end of himself. He didn't beg or shout at God to do something; he simply gave himself and his problem over into the Lord's hands. And God didn't let him down. He didn't agree it was all a bit of a foolish waste of time, or a big mistake (as the world tells us), but He told Elijah to go back the way he came, retrace all those painful, disillusioned steps, and just do two or three small jobs – anoint two kings and pick his prophetic successor. And Elijah responded to God's commands.

Elijah walked on and came to Elisha, who was ploughing with twelve oxen. As soon as Elijah threw his mantle over him, Elisha knew what he had come for, as if God had already prepared him for this moment. But there was a time gap between the promise and the fulfilment. So, it is worth noting that if we receive a prophecy that we are to have a healing ministry, it does not necessarily mean it will happen immediately. The prophecy does not produce the ministry; our anointing and our obedience to God produce that. There may be an intermediate period of testing and discipline when God often reveals what is hidden in our hearts.

Elisha did go back home, but only to prove that he was completely dedicated to follow Elijah. He kissed his mother and father good-bye and:

> ...He took his yoke of oxen and slaughtered them. He burned the ploughing equipment, to cook the meat and gave it to the people, and they ate. Then he set out to follow Elijah and became his attendant (1 Kings 19:21).

He made a public statement that there was to be no safety net in case it didn't work, no regrets. He was determined to have what Elijah had, no matter what it cost.

In 2 Kings 2, the Lord is about to take Elijah up to heaven in a whirlwind, and Elisha knows it. Imagine how he felt when Elijah turned to him and said, "Stay here, the Lord has sent me to Bethel, stay at Gilgal."

After all they have been through, is Elijah rejecting him? Elisha could have taken it like that, but instead he saw it as a test of his dedication and faith.

166

He swears not to leave his master. Then the whole of the company of prophets come out and ask, "Do you know that the Lord is going to take your master from you today?"

And Elisha replies curtly, "Yes I know, but do not speak of it. Hold your peace; I don't want your discouragement, I don't want your information, I don't want to get sidetracked. My eyes aren't on what's going to happen, they're on Elijah, and I'm going wherever he goes."

Now Bethel is the first place inside the Promised Land. It was the place where Jacob met with God and had an angelic visitation; the place where God met with him and he worshipped God. Elijah offering Elisha the option to stay where he was, if you like: stay here and worship God here; but I am going to another place in the land, Elisha had his eyes on his master and followed him.

So Elijah and Elisha went on to Jericho, the place of faith. It wasn't just a miracle place. It was a place of faith. For six days, two million people walked round the walls once a day without murmuring. That was a miracle in itself. Can you imagine what it did to the enemy? They were all on the walls looking down, wondering what on earth these people were doing walking around without a sound. And on the seventh day, when they all gave a huge shout, the shock was so great, the walls fell down. It was a victory of faith and obedience. Elisha was determined to go on into a deeper realm with God. Again he received more discouragement for he got the same treatment from the prophets at Jericho. And once more, he gave them the same short answer.

Finally, Elijah declared he was going on to Jordan, the place of death, and he urged Elisha to stay at Jericho, the place of faith. But having come this far, Elisha was not going to miss what he had set his heart upon, no matter what it cost, so the two of them went on to the banks of the Jordan. Then Elijah took his coat, rolled it up and struck the water with it, and the water divided so that they were able to cross over on dry ground. And when they crossed, Elijah said to Elisha, "Tell me, what can I do for you before I am taken from you?"

And Elisha replied quickly, "Let me inherit a double portion of your spirit."

This was the vision, the goal, which had fuelled his dedication all along. Elijah said, "You have asked a difficult thing."

"Yet if you see me when I am taken from you," continues Elijah "it will be yours – otherwise not."

This is the crux of the matter in the healing ministry. Where we fix our eyes, what will our attention be on? Will we be looking at the supernatural events and desire to perform them? Will we look at the hopelessness and need of so many sick people and be daunted in our faith? Or will we concentrate on the God with whom nothing is impossible? I found in the early years of my healing ministry that I could pray for anything I could not see. If people looked healthy, that was fine, but it they looked as if they were dying on their feet, I found it very difficult to pray with any confidence. At first it was OK because I tried not to notice people who looked really sick, but then God began to bring the crippled, the maimed, the deformed, the handicapped – and I cried to the Lord, "Help me I need more faith." And He said simply, "Seek Me." That didn't seem like a solution at all so I thought of going to the Morris Cerullo Annual Convention.

"Seek Me," He said again.

…Or maybe I could go and see Kathryn Kuhlman. Some friend had offered to pay my fare to America so that I could attend one of her meetings and I was joyful. All I needed was a visa. So I went to the American Embassy and was told basically, "You haven't got a job, you reckon to live by faith (crazy), we don't want you in America." Three times I returned to the embassy and three times I was refused an entry visa.

I was staying in the house of friends at the time and on the day before I was meant to fly, the lady of the house came over to me and said, "I believe I have a word from the Lord for you. 'Your appointment is not with a man, not with a woman, but with me,' saith the Lord. Good night!"

I knew that I could not go to bed until I prayed through this, so I stayed up far into the night praying and asking God what was going on. Then at about three in the morning a light appeared in the room and suddenly Jesus stood before me. In an instant I hit the ground at His feet, and the spirit of God surged through me like a mighty tidal wave that it was impossible even to pray in tongues. I was groaning, yet without any sound, and the only word which escaped was, "Lord, Lord…"

Then Jesus spoke to me and said. "In that day you will know that I am in you and you are in Me!"

That day I did know it. That day I knew that Jesus Christ was alive, and alive in me. I didn't know it because the Scriptures said so, or because it was church doctrine, but because I had actually seen Him.

The next morning, I went to the embassy, saw the same clerk, and was granted a visa without any trouble. I discovered at the same time that all the previous day's planes had been grounded by fog for twenty-four hours, so I was able to use the same Apex ticket I got for the day before. I went straight to the huge Morris Cerullo convention in California where there was a great sense of the anointing of God. In fact, there were people in the convention who prayed for the sick, and when they came forward they received a special anointing from the Lord. Everyone went running down, and he took one look at me and exclaimed, "Brother, I can't pray for you, you've already got it!"

The next thing I knew we had all collapsed on the ground under the power of God. So I never did receive it from a man.

From San Diego, I flew to Ohio to the Kathryn Kuhlman service and I sat there minding my own business, just praying desperately that she would receive a word of knowledge, like "There is someone here from England who stammers…" When suddenly she pointed her finger in our direction and said, "There are some people here from England. Stand up." Hardly able to believe it, my two friends and I responded immediately. Then she said to us:

"Come up on to the stage." We went up in a kind of daze.

"Tell me," she said to me, "What do YOU do?" I could hardly speak for a moment. My mind was reeling.

"I've got a hhhhhh-healing ministry," I stuttered.

"W-o-n-d-e-r-f-u-l," she replied.

She went on to explain that the Lord had told her He was going to send people from all over the world because He wanted the healing ministry to expand everywhere. Then came the crunch:

"Do you want more of God or would you like to be healed?"

Now what can you say in front of thousands of people? God had set me up magnificently! If I had been like Elisha, I would have said, "Both," but I did not have the nerve. I said, "More of God," thank you.

My ministry was enlarged from that day. When I returned to England,

I found I was praying for the seriously ill and the crippled. I could actually feel deformed limbs and bodies straightening out as I closed my eyes and reached out to the Lord, and when I looked, they were completely restored to wholeness; healed and good as new. I was amazed! It had to be the anointing!

So let us return to Elijah and Elisha. "You can have the double portion, if you see me go up."

This was to be the final test of Elisha's single-mindedness and commitment. Would he be distracted by the spectacular events God would produce, or would he keep his eyes on Elijah?

> *As they were walking along and talking together, suddenly a chariot of fire and horses of fire appeared and separated the two of them, and Elijah went up to heaven in a whirlwind* (2 Kings 2:11).

If I had seen horses of fire – a whirlwind and chariots of fire zooming through the sky like a divine sledge – I'm quite sure I would have taken a look at it, particularly as these heavenly messengers actually drove between them and parted them just as they were enjoying a quiet conversation together. Nothing could have prepared Elisha for moment. Suddenly he was on his own. But he kept his eyes on Elijah:

> *"...My father! My father! The chariots and horsemen of Israel!..."*
> (2 Kings 2:12).

And Elisha saw him no more.

When my wife and I went to another Kathryn Kuhlman meeting, I thought at the start that I was going to miss out on all the blessings because a huge concrete pillar obstructed me. When Kathryn Kuhlman walked on to the stage, I could not even see her. I was getting very frustrated as I tried to lean first one way and then the other to catch a glimpse of what was going on: "Lord," I cried out, "I can't see a thing."

"Don't worry, I put you there," He replied.

"Why? Don't you love me?" Just as I asked this, Kathryn Kuhlman's voice rang out: "Second row in the balcony, there's a person there who is being healed of a brain tumour." It was the woman next to me. Just the other side of me somebody else was healed of epilepsy. She went down the row and missed me because I was hidden behind this wretched pillar. I was wild with impatience. Peeping out from behind the pillar, I looked down resentfully at everyone below, and thought, I expect that all those Christians in the front row come from this city of Pittsburgh, and they come for this every week. I have travelled almost five thousand miles and I can't even get a decent seat. I am glad God has gifts for the rebellious!

He said to me, "It is alright. I have you sitting in this seat for a reason."

"But I can't see Miss Kuhlman," I almost shouted.

"That was my intention," replied the Lord.

Then, a few seconds later, an extraordinary thing happened. I could almost physically see the person of the Holy Spirit. Somehow I could see Him moving right across on the far side of the church and a moment later Kathryn Kuhlman said, "God is moving over there now, and somebody is being healed." And I knew what they were being healed. So I asked the Lord what He was showing me. And He said, "Do you see the miracles, or do you see the God who does them? For only those who see the God who does the miracles can actually move in this realm themselves."

This is how the double portion functions, looking away from the signs and wonders and keeping your eyes firmly on the God who works miracles. Elisha saw Elijah go up alive into the heavens. He hung on to the end. He needed no further word or commission. The contract had been fulfilled on both sides. Now he had only to receive. So he picked up Elijah's cloak, went back to the Jordan and struck the water, fully expecting it to part. Hundreds of years before Christ, Elisha illustrated the reality of the miraculous ministry which is available to us if we steadfastly look to Jesus, allowing our own lives to be used so that we can pick up the mantle of His anointing.

For Jesus said,

> *"Believe me when I say that I am in the Father and the Father is in me; or at least believe on the evidence of the miracles themselves. I tell you the truth, anyone who has faith in me will do what I have been doing. He will do even greater works than these, because I am going to the Father. And I will do whatever you ask in my name, so that the Son may bring glory to the Father. **You may ask for anything in my name and I will do it***" (John 14:11-14 [emphasis added]).

It sounds wonderful, does it not? Who does not want to do greater works than Jesus? Let us all be where the action is. But it was Kathryn Kuhlman who once said "There is nothing God has given me that He won't give to you, if you are prepared to pay the price."

Had I envisaged what being a disciple would mean, I might never have signed up in the first place. However this is what discipleship is about - doing the work of the Lord. If we are faithful in small things, the Scriptures promise us greater rewards. We must expect to make mistakes, we all do, but be encouraged, it is better to pray for ten people and have one healed than not to pray at all.

Peter had more failures than any of the other disciples: he tried to walk on the water and nearly sank; he fell asleep at the transfiguration; he fell asleep in Gethsemane; he cut off the ear of the high priest's servant; he even denied Christ. I think most of us would have given up if we had made a mess of things that often. But Peter accepted the death of his pride, and so God was able to exalt him. Through all his mistakes, Peter's heart was right. He wanted to serve Christ no matter what it cost, and significantly it was to him, and not to John the contemplative, the apostle of love, for example that God gave the revelation of the nature of Jesus. And in response to Peter's declaration of faith, Jesus promised him:

> ...*Blessed are you, Simon [meaning a reed], son of Jonah, for this was not revealed to you by man, but by my Father in heaven. And I tell you that you are Peter, [a rock], and on this rock I will build my church, and the gates of Hades will not overcome it. I will give you the keys of the kingdom of heaven; and whatever you bind on earth will be bound in heaven, and whatever you loose on earth will be loosed in heaven* (Matthew 16:17-19).

Then on the day of Pentecost, we see Peter entering into the fullness of his ministry, preaching to thousands, healing the sick, and establishing the church. But God made him go the first mile. He paid the price, and he paid it all through his life, with persecution and suffering, eventually a terrible martyrdom, but he kept his faith just as Jesus promised him.

> *Simon, Simon, Satan has asked to sift you as wheat. But I have prayed for you, Simon, that your faith may not fail...* (Luke 22:31; 32).

Just as He changed water into wine, Jesus can transform the weak water of our natural lives into the rich, full wine of His supernatural life. And just as the master of the banquet tasted the wine, so God samples the quality of the life within us to see whether the bouquet carries the fragrance of Jesus, looking for the fullness and strength of the life of Christ. It may be that the wine of our lives needs more time to mature. The cloudiness and impurities of our inner selves must be refined until the glory of Jesus alone shines through us. For "We, who with unveiled faces all reflect the Lord's glory, are being transformed into his likeness with ever-increasing glory, which comes from the Lord, who is the Spirit" (2 Corinthians 3:18).

And the glory is the Lord's. We must be so careful never to claim it for ourselves. If the power of God heals people through us, it has nothing to do with our ability or spirituality. It is simply that we have decreased so that He might increase; it is that we have died so that His life might come through us. If we commit ourselves to that double portion and pay the price, God's grace will draw us into an ever-deeper experience of His power and love, so that we, too, can say to the Lord: "Everyone brings out the choice wine first, and then the cheaper wine after the guests have had too much to drink; but you have saved the best till now" (John 2:10).

# Bibliography

Bosworth, F.F. Christ the Healer. 9th Edition. Grand Rapids: Baker, 1924, 2001.

Copeland, Kenneth. John G. Lake: His Life, His Sermons, His Boldness of Faith. Tulsa: Harrison House, 1996.

Hagin, Kenneth. Redeemed from Poverty, Sickness and Death. Tulsa: Kenneth Hagin Ministries.

Liardon, Roberts. God's Generals: Why They Succeeded and Some Failed. Tulsa: Albury Publishing 1996.

McCrossan, Dr. T.J. Bodily Healing in the Atonement. 2nd edition. Tulsa OK: Kenneth Hagin Ministries.

McNutt, Francis. The Prayer That Heals: Praying for Healing in the Family. Notre Dame: Ave Maria Press, 1984.

_____. Healing. Revised and Expanded. Notre Dame: Ave Maria Press, 1999.

Osborn, T.L. Healing the Sick. A Living Classic. Tulsa: Harrison House, 1986.

Sandford, John & Paula. The Transformation of the Inner Man. Tulsa: Victory Publishing House.

Sandford, John & Paula. Healing The Wounded Spirit. Tulsa: Victory Publishing House.

To contact Dr Ian Andrews

ian@equippers.org

ian@citadelministries.com

Printed in Great Britain
by Amazon

33392841R00102